Rallying

A practical guide to
successful competition

Chris Sclater & Martin Holmes

FABER & FABER : 3 Queen Square : London

Rallying

In the same series
JUDO
by George Glass
TABLE TENNIS
by Harold Myers

First published in 1977 by Faber and Faber Limited
3 Queen Square, London WC1N 3AU
Set by Filmtype Services Limited
Printed and bound in Great Britain by
Redwood Burn Limited, Trowbridge & Esher
All rights reserved

ACKNOWLEDGEMENTS

The authors are grateful to the following for
permission to reproduce photographs in which
they hold the copyright: Hugh W. Bishop, British
Leyland Motor Corporation Ltd., Esler Crawford
Photography, John L. E. Gaisford, Dave Gray,
F. E. Hall, Peter Meininger, Tony North, Roger Swan,
Colin Taylor Productions.

British Library Cataloguing Publication Data

Sclater, Chris
    Rallying.
    1. Automobile rallies
    I. Title   II. Holmes, Martin, b.1940
    796.7'2   GV1029.2

ISBN 0-571-11000-2

Contents

Foreword by Mike Greasley p. 6

1 *A week in the life of a rally driver* p. 7
Chris Sclater

2 *Co-driving as a way of life* p. 16
Martin Holmes

3 *So you want to be a rally driver?* p. 25
Chris Sclater

4 *Beginnings for a co-driver* p. 32
Martin Holmes

5 *Is sideways safest?* p. 41
Chris Sclater

6 *Rules and regulations, and rallies
in general* p. 53
Martin Holmes

7 *Be prepared* p. 62
Chris Sclater

8 *Frightened?* p. 73
Martin Holmes

9 *From theory to practice* p. 82
Martin Holmes

10 *Foreign rallies* p. 97
Chris Sclater

11 *Confidence* p. 108
Martin Holmes

12 *Teams* p. 119
Chris Sclater

Foreword

The first time I met Chris Sclater and Martin Holmes was on the Dukeries Rally way back in 1971. It was my first event as a reporter for *Motoring News*, and I must have looked even more lost and confused than I do today because Chris and Martin quickly befriended me, offering advice and explanations and stories. Since then I have become a firm friend of them both, still relying on their invaluable comments and advice. When Datsun asked me to become Team Manager it was therefore an obvious move to get them in the team. It was a decision which was based not only on their complete understanding of rallying, but also on the fact that as a pair they are an ideal combination in a rally car, a pair on whom a harassed team manager could rely completely. I wasn't to be disappointed.

Now they embark on their first book together, a joint exercise which I find a fund of useful information, tips and advice for everyone whether at the top of the ladder or taking first tentative steps up from the bottom – a book which has proved to me that I've still got a lot to learn.

Mike Greasley

MIKE GREASLEY · WORTHING

Illustrations on facing page: Recceing for a foreign international
Checking on car preparation at the garage
Contact with the media. Martin is interviewed by BBC's 'Wheelbase'

1 *A week in the life of a rally driver*
By CHRIS SCLATER

Monday morning, nine o'clock and the phone rings. 'Ford Motor Company here – can you spend Friday instructing at our rally school at Castle Donington? We'll send you details but please be there at nine o'clock.' This is a good start to the week. Somebody offering employment – employment which involves driving. The more driving a rally driver does the better. An obvious comment perhaps, but a rally driver spends very little of his time actually rally driving. The rest of the week proves that.

I don't have 'typical' weeks. In fact since I gave up a regular job in 1971 I have not spent two similar weeks. I will outline the sort of activities the full-time rally driver is involved in and relate them to my own life.

Following the call from Fords I was on the phone for an hour or so making arrangements for an International Rally in northern Spain. A chat with the clerk of the course established facts which were important to a competitor but particularly important to somebody from

7

England. Were there any companies interested in sponsoring a leading competitor? Were there concessions on hotel accommodation? Did any shipping company give a discount for the boat crossing?

Next a call to my travel agent. 'I want to transport a service car and trailer plus two people to the north coast of Spain – by the cheapest way. And please book a ticket for a car and two people on the channel crossing' (that would be for me and my co-driver with a recce car). The rally car and service car must go by the least arduous route, but the recce car by the cheapest. With two people aboard driving through France this cost less than half the price of air tickets, with the added advantage of saving the cost of a hire car for the recce.

The insurance man came next – green card and bail bonds for three cars with four named drivers. 'We need their ages, occupations and driving experience.' Another phone call. After checking the route in the regulations, tyre requirements could be worked out and the order was put in by phone to Goodyear Racing Division: ten racing tyres and sixteen rough road tyres.

A lunchtime meeting with a potential sponsor followed, but at the last moment before leaving the house I remembered to take some casual clothes as I would be dropping in at the garage afterwards. The sponsor was politely interested but I knew that the chances of a successful deal with him were slim. Still, I couldn't afford to leave any stones unturned.

To the garage after lunch. Brian Ashwood was working on the rally car. I changed and helped him. We were trying a new suspension modification, although with scheduled rebuilding work to be done this was a bit of a luxury. I worked there until seven o'clock and then drove home (thirty miles outside London). After something to eat I got down to writing an article for *Motor* magazine, to which I contribute.

A fairly typical Monday, but I could just as easily have been in Portugal recceing for the Portuguese Rally or in the Isle of Man for the Manx. Wherever I was I would have been hard at work – in fact only people who have practised for a rally realize just how hard the work is. Sitting in a standard car, usually with a standard seat, driving over bumpy roads from daylight to darkness, concentrating on driving smoothly so that your co-driver can write fairly neatly, and making good pace notes, is a tiring business. You must concentrate on the driving, make accurate pace notes – and try to forget about a long cool beer or the beautiful view. The recce could be a few days or, in the case of the Monte Carlo Rally, a few weeks. Very tedious but very important.

Another important part of professional competition is contact with the media. From time to time there are test days arranged so that the Press can see what rallying is all about. On these days I take the rally car to a test track and together with other drivers and manufacturers demonstrate to the Press and television the merits of the car or just the merits of rallying. Lack of captive spectators is one of the major problems of rallying and education of the Press is the best way to encourage spectator interest. Usually these days are very worth while and those members of the Press who allow themselves to be chauffeured around a 'special stage' go away amazed and exhilarated.

With a national rally coming up at the weekend, I spent Wednesday working on the rally car helping with the final preparations – arranging for the paint spraying which usually has to be done before every event to make sure that the car is smart. The sign-writer also had to be booked to deal with the advertising on the car. The tyres would be ready to collect from Goodyear at Watford, so I would take the service car to pick them up. I had to be back home relatively early to be able to go out to a motor club forum where I was on the panel with another driver, a co-driver and a tyre expert. A lively evening, thanks to the audience which usually makes or breaks this sort of function.

Thursday morning was taken up finishing off the article and delivering it to the magazine offices, followed by some phoning to confirm hotels for the weekend and chase up the arrangements for the rally in Spain. I remembered to order some special brake pads from Ferodo. After lunch it was back to the garage to see how the car was getting on. Two hours' work and it was ready for the test drive. This involved my driving out of London checking the engine for performance, temperatures and oil leaks, bedding in brakes and generally making sure that nothing silly was wrong with the car. After driving for about an hour I returned to the garage to check everything and start loading up: rally car on the trailer, all the spares and wheels in the service car.

Friday morning I was up early (five o'clock) to drive to Donington Park for the rally school. Pupils would be arriving just before nine and the school started with a film at nine ten. Practical instruction would be from ten to four with an hour for lunch. I had six pupils and we used an Escort 1600 supplied by Fords. The idea was for me to drive each pupil round a simulated special stage and then change over and try to teach him from the passenger seat. It is a very satisfying experience – if

Rally school instruction

a bit hair-raising at times – to be able to pass on some driving skills to people who can make use of them. At the end of the day I felt shattered, but happy to have a few pounds for the effort.

Meanwhile Brian and Terry Samuell were on their way to Glasgow with the rally car, and I set off north to meet them at the hotel. I got there soon after nine that evening and enjoyed a drink with them and a good meal. Martin Holmes arrived and joined us. Scrutineering for the rally was at eleven o'clock on Saturday morning and we were up at eight to unload the car, park the trailer in a garage, sort out the spares, fit the correct tyres for the first part of the rally, put on the competition numbers and clean off the motorway dirt. We went down to the scrutineering and passed through the formalities without any problems. At this point Martin collected the details of the route for the

Service point (1975 Scottish Rally; Datsun Violet)

event. It started that evening at nine and finished at midday on Sunday. He started putting the route on the map and working out the schedule for Brian and Terry in the service car. I had a good lunch and then went to bed to stock up on sleep.

Up at eight o'clock that evening, I changed into driving overalls, had a snack with Martin and then took the car up to the start. Brian had already set off with the service car to his first service point where we would see him about ten-thirty. This rally followed the usual pattern of British national events. The competitive part took place on forest roads which were laid out as special stages. They were closed to other traffic and we had to try to achieve a sixty-mile-an-hour average speed –

usually impossible because of the nature of the road. This rally had two stages on tarmac. One was a hill-climb and the other a disused airfield. We had to change on to racing tyres for these two. Goodyear have put their racing experience to good use and have produced an excellent version suitable for rallying.

The rally went well. It took a pattern of special stages each followed by a service stop with liaison sections on the public road which varied between a couple of miles up to perhaps twenty or thirty. At four o'clock on Sunday morning we all wondered what on earth we were doing in the middle of some forest when it would be better to be curled up asleep between clean sheets. The body is at its low about this time, but by seven o'clock things felt better and a breakfast stop at eight made the world look a good deal brighter.

We were lying in fourth position at breakfast time and there were only five stages left. As is usual on these events, the top places were very closely contended, with only seconds separating the first half-dozen. But things didn't change to the finish despite the fact that a rear brake caliper broke on the penultimate stage. Luckily the last stage had few corners so the breakage didn't make more than a few seconds' difference.

The rally was over, although for the co-driver the job of checking all the times – ours and our competitors' – was just beginning. Martin was busy until the results were announced and ultimately declared final. For the rest of us lunch was top priority, followed by a few hours' sleep before the prize-giving party in the evening. The party was typical. Too many people trying to buy drinks from a badly understaffed bar and a lot of tall-story swapping – 'There I was with eight thousand on the clock levelling out at three feet when this tree jumped out. . . .' It's at times like this we wish that rallying was less of a male-dominated occupation.

After the prize-giving, which inevitably was late, the party started to break up. Most people were either making a start homeward straight away or getting up early in the morning as we were. Back at the hotel there were a group of drivers and mechanics putting the world to rights in a sleepy sort of a way, and we were quite happy to join them. Martin, poor chap, had to start typing his story of the rally for a magazine. The residents' bar closed at one, sending us all to bed. Monday morning saw us up at seven, loading up the rally car and winding our laborious way back down the motorways into London.

So ended a random week for me. But just as easily it could have been spent driving on the Total Rally in South Africa, the Scottish Rally or the Rothmans Rally in Jamaica. It could have been spent in the garage working all hours to sort out an engine failure, or tyre and suspension testing in mid-Wales.

I remember one of the most hectic weeks of my career was a few years ago when I drove in three different types of motor sport in a week. An international rally in Spain finished on Friday and was followed by a very rapid lift to Madrid airport to fly back to England early Saturday morning. I had to go straight to the garage to pick up a rallycross car and travel to Long Marston near Stratford-on-Avon for a televised rallycross meeting. Then I went down to Thruxton to drive a Mexico in a six-hour relay race. All three events were fairly successful, and if I remember correctly we were the second team on handicap in the relay race which won us a gallon of Duckhams each and a year's subscription to *Cars and Car Conversions* magazine!

When your life is committed to motor sport the driving is a minority occupation. There are few people who earn their entire living from driving alone. Roger Clark has a garage business, Timo Makinen has a boat-building factory, Simo Lampinen makes skis. Hannu Mikkola is one of the very few who does nothing apart from rallying.

So don't seek your fortune behind the wheel of a rally car; but success can lead you into other fields which are connected to motor sport. I have earned money from some surprising activities. The most unusual was supplying the soundtrack for the car that Edward Fox drove in *The Day of the Jackal*. The sound editor wanted a more sporting note to put on the Alfa Romeo in the film. I was asked to take my Escort BDA to Blackbushe airport for two days where we copied the exact movements and timings of the car in the film. The recorded sounds were dubbed on to the picture – complete with the rattle of the ZF gearbox. The payment was not in the Richard Burton category but it certainly paid the rent for a few weeks.

I was also involved in a commercial film for a brand of cigarettes to be shown in Malaysia. The theme of the film was a bit corny. Our hero is seen racing over a special stage and sliding across the finishing line the winner, only to reach nonchalantly for a pack of Brand X filter-tip cigarettes. I did the driving and an actor was substituted for the finish. We went to Eppynt ranges in Wales with an Escort and a few other cars as background, co-opted some troops who happened to be on man-oeuvres to act as crowd, and did some fairly exciting things, including flying the Escort over the camera and deliberately driving through a wall of straw bales.

Journalism has also become one of my activities. I have written a regular column in *Motor*, a chapter in the *Triple C Book of Rallying*, articles for a magazine in South Africa, and have even written the script for a film Lombard made of the RAC Rally – not only writing the script, but speaking the commentary as well. This was a very interesting project and also hard work – the processes involved in making a film are more complicated than I had ever imagined. Considering I only scraped through English Language at school, this involvement with writing has surprised me more than anyone else!

Before the Monte in 1973 I was asked by Holts – the car accessory people – to help in the promotion of a new product. I had to carry stickers on the car for the rally, not the usual advertising but small paint patches which were almost invisible, and were designed to cover rust spots and other blemishes. The idea was to show how these 'scratch patches', as they were called, would stand up to rigorous

12

Rallycrossing (240 Z at Long Marston, 1974)

motoring conditions. After the rally I took the car along to the Mermaid Theatre in the City to appear in the official launch of the new product.

All these non-driving activities can pay. How much depends on how hard you are in the dealing. But undoubtedly an important part of the modern rally driver's activities, whether he is professional or not, is connected with promotional work. Sometimes this is self-promotion, but more usual are the promotional activities for sponsors. These are normally part of the deal made with the sponsor in the first place, and can range from opening new garages, appearing in stores for the launch of a new product, celebrity evenings with motor clubs, and talks to such unlikely groups as the Women's Institute or the Rotary Club – all of which I have done.

One of the more bizarre jobs I undertook was for Ford before the World Cup Rally in 1970. Because of late snow, the actual crews driving on the event had not managed to look at one of the special stages in

Relay race at Thruxton (Mexico team, 1972)

Yugoslavia. Stuart Turner phoned me out of the blue and in his usual to-the-point manner suggested that I could prove myself and earn some money into the bargain by looking over this stage for them. The idea was to go to Split on the Adriatic coast, hire a car, drive over the stage and return to meet the rally cars before the stage. The other job was to make pace notes into a tape recorder, and copy out six sets. As it turned out, this was certainly going to be a Turner initiative test.

Bill Barnett, then Ford's co-ordinator at Boreham, had fixed the air tickets to Zagreb and the connecting flight on to Split. I was to collect them at the airport. When I arrived at the BEA ticket desk at the terminal – no air tickets. Luckily there was space on the plane and they accepted my personal cheque. The flight was an hour late taking off, which meant I missed the last connecting flight to Split. It was Saturday evening. The rally was due to arrive on Wednesday, so time was short. I had to get to Split as soon as possible. My only possibility was a night sleeper train, which I just caught with a few minutes to spare. Arriving in Split at five o'clock on Sunday morning, with little cash, only travellers' cheques, was certainly not very much like the start of an Adriatic holiday. The next problem was to find a hire car. Arriving on Sunday instead of Saturday posed a problem – the hire car offices didn't open on Sunday. I had to knock up the manager of the Avis office and persuade him to hire me a car. I was successful and eventually drove off into the mountains in a rather tatty Peugeot 204.

The start of the stage was about a hundred and fifty kilometres away over rough roads, and after about fifty I had a puncture. Next snag – the spare was soft. I had a few pounds of pressure, however, and I drove on slowly to the next village and borrowed a foot pump. I reached Glamoc, the town at the start of the stage, in the evening, and booked into the only hotel which was about half a star. Early on Monday morning I had the puncture repaired and set off up the stage. The country was very wild and there were still traces of snow on the muddy tracks of the stage. I was holding the microphone of the tape recorder and making pace notes while driving. The total length was two hundred kilometres and at ninety-three kilometres I had another puncture. This time the spare was flat; the valve must have been leaking.

On the map there was no village for another fifty kilometres and that only very small. There was little possibility of hitching a lift since I hadn't seen another vehicle all day. If I went back down the stage I could turn off on to a tarmac road quite soon, and presumably have more chance of finding help. So I put the punctured wheel on the back (the 204 is front-wheel drive) and set off singing 'Three Wheels on my Wagon'.

After thirty kilometres the tyre disappeared and the wheel was like an old three-penny bit. So I thought it would be a good idea to put the punctured spare on! After another twenty kilometres I reached a village – but no garage, and certainly no spare tyre, let alone a wheel. It was clear that I wouldn't be able to finish my recce of the stage but at least I knew the snow had gone and had made some pace notes. I had to get back to Glamoc as soon as possible. It was Monday afternoon.

I found a man who could give me a lift some of the way down the road. When he dropped me at his destination I started walking. . . . I assumed I would be able to hitch a lift. It turned out that it is illegal to pick up hitch-hikers in Yugoslavia, so fifteen kilometres later I was still walking and thinking about charging Stuart Turner for a new pair of shoes. Eventually a French family on holiday gave me a lift to the next village and dropped me at the bus stop where I caught a bus into the nearest town. Nobody spoke English or French, only German, and as they say, 'I didn't have any German'.

I stayed the night there and the hotel manager eventually understood that I needed a taxi to go to Glamoc. No taxi would take me as the journey was over rough roads and quite a long way. The manager then found a friend who would take me in his private car. He wanted the equivalent of £25 and all I could offer was about £20 – which to my relief he accepted. It was about a hundred kilometres to Glamoc and, being concerned about damaging his car, he drove at about twenty-five kilometres an hour the whole way – stopping at every village for a coffee. We reached Glamoc on Tuesday evening, and when one of the Goodyear mechanics appeared from the hotel and asked if I'd had a good trip, I didn't know whether to laugh or cry.

I wrote out the pace notes on Wednesday and the rally passed through that night. Apparently, on the stage at a point beyond my puncture, a bridge was broken and the cars had to retrace their steps a few kilometres to go round it. When I returned to England the only comment that Stuart Turner made was: 'Pity you didn't reach the bridge.' I didn't even try to explain! As Michael Frostick said to me once: 'Take the cheque and shut up.'

2 *Co-driving as a way of life*
By MARTIN HOLMES

Running through a cold, wet forest searching for spectators to help you heave your rally car back on to the track is not perhaps the most attractive occupation, but the life of co-driving has a variety of aspects. For every time you are invited to sit in a clean, new rally car to try out the seating position and check that every instrument is within easy reach there is another occasion when you curse the very existence of rally cars. Just once in a while things happen in a way which makes every little discomfort or uncertainty worth while; you win an event or you pull some magic surprise out of the bag: these are the good moments, the moments you will recall in the years to come. What, though, is a co-driver's life like as a whole?

Co-driving is a sport you can enjoy at many different levels. Obviously the great majority enjoy it as a pastime, a weekend occupation with the opportunity to compete on occasion for longer periods. Even the British professional co-drivers are able to go rallying with a regular permanent employment outside the sport. Obviously a lot of spare time will be taken up with making arrangements, with paperwork, with promotional work and with understanding regulations, but this essentially is evening work. Very few co-drivers in Britain expect to earn anything more than money to defray their expenses, and until you as a co-driver have achieved successes in the past you cannot even expect to pay your way. At higher levels the financial involvement increases at a fast rate, and as soon as you enter the areas of the sport where you spend time that otherwise would be used for earning a living you have to examine this aspect very carefully.

Later in this chapter we will look at the life of a professional co-driver, and also the life of people who rally abroad, where the nature of rallies demands that a lot of time is spent actually on the job. Even now there is a reluctance to take the work of a co-driver as seriously as the co-drivers themselves feel is justified, and this means that you have to be especially good at the job before people regard you as anything more than just another enthusiast who enjoys the sport.

What makes a person want to co-drive in the first place? To me, the enjoyment in rallying is primarily that of being driven by people able to drive at far faster speeds than I could manage. Secondly, it is the satisfaction of commanding a team and harnessing the skill of a driver

Left: A navigator must be a useful person to have around (Johnstone Syer)

Right: Checking and cross-checking – you must be trusted to get things right: Jean Todt at work

into successful rallying. These two aspects produce the satisfaction that excuses hours and hours of hard work. Other benefits from the sport are simply by-products to these main factors. A lot of other people go co-driving for other reasons: travel is a prime motivating factor, the opportunity to be involved in an exciting scene is another, and for a few it is the opportunity to prove themselves as drivers in their own right.

As a job co-driving has nothing in its favour; there is no future, there is little or no money in the work, there is an element (though fortunately a very small element) of danger and a considerable element of discomfort. As a sport it does not even have the compensation of being a way of earning a living. Rallying is obviously a sport pure and simple, a method of proving oneself to be better than a rival, and co-driving is an essential part of the sport. Drivers and mechanics need a reliable co-driver just as much as a co-driver needs a reliable driver and mechanics. You are part of a team.

What makes a useful co-driver? Essentially you must be a useful person to have around, useful in the sense of being reliable and knowledgeable in your work, and equally important, useful in the sense of being willing and helpful, and intelligent enough to grasp situations as and when they arise. Like wine, co-drivers usually get better as they grow older. The more rallies they enter, the more things they know about the sport. Experience pays off in a million ways. You learn about the places where rallies go; the laybys at the side of the road where the mechanics can wait for you; the nasty corners that the maps do not show; hundreds of little techniques which can save you time on the special stages or save you from a serious tactical error; the methods of doing things which will stop you from getting tired unnecessarily; and how rivals will react to circumstances. But all these attributes are of little benefit unless you, as a co-driver, are motivated by a desire to do as well as possible.

On one occasion Chris Sclater and I finished a rally and there was trouble with the organizers over various times for the stages. Chris was tired and fed up with my continual enquiries as to how far we should press the organizers to correct the errors. In the end he said that he had done his job, would I now please do mine and tell him when we had won!

I believe you can tell a really good co-driver by the way he studies the provisional results of a rally: a good co-driver is the one who checks and re-checks the results even when he only stands to come tenth overall. Whereas drivers are judged almost entirely by the results which they are capable of attaining, co-drivers are judged by a variety of other factors. You must be trusted to get things right, to create no aggro and essentially to let a driver concentrate on his job of driving.

Why is rallying in Britain only a part-time sport? Basically because the rallies are short and there are hardly any events in Britain that demand more than four or five days' work, even for professionals. Drivers have a greater opportunity for work, for they have to test cars and often they are involved with development, but co-drivers simply have to make their preparations and attend on the day. Even major companies do not plan more than ten to fifteen events in a year, and consequently should you seek full-time employment as a co-driver you must be prepared to carry out a lot of work which is only marginally related to the actual sport. Publicity is the usual activity that marries up with the work of a driver, and, of course, this leads to the natural inference that professional rally men have to be masters of more than just one trade.

Rallying abroad, which will be described in later chapters, can be a full-time job. Rallies abroad demand a minimum of one week's preparation, and some of the big world championship events demand two or three. Whereas a British full-time co-driver will only find himself rallying for some seventy-five days in a year, a continental expert will be occupied for a hundred and fifty to two hundred days. In years gone by, British companies made the leading continental rallies their major objective, and for a British co-driver this was an ideal situation. With the recent economic difficulties this level of activity declined, and has now reached such a low that the outlook for the future can only be favourable.

This lack of British events brings with it another problem. These events have become extremely competitive. Reliability and the ability to handle fatigue have become matters of minor importance, and consequently the fastest cars win every time. This means that the only way a driver can remain in the limelight is to be winning, and to be winning he has to drive one of the fastest cars. The Ford Escort has for some time been the winning car, and as there have been very few vacancies to drive these cars professionally potential professional drivers have had to drive cars of other manufacturers – cars which generally start off at a disadvantage. To win in Britain, you sometimes have to pay for your sport. To be a professional driver in Britain means you must be prepared to lose, however hard you drive. This situation affects co-drivers, since at the present state of the sport, you cannot expect private teams to give you professional rides; so your only opportunities will lie in rides on potential class-winning cars. This can give you rides in all the major events, but it will bring a hankering and a wistfulness for a chance to ride in a winning car. Until classes become of comparable importance to overall positions, all you will be thinking about are the thirty-nine or so amateur co-drivers who are beating you every time.

```
MAZMO TUN WELLS
814571 FSO PL        TEOELEX NR 355/76   12. 01. 76R.

   ATTATION MR . MARIN HOLMES

ON  XXNXXXX JANUARY THE 10- TH OUR MECHANIC TESTED YOUR CAR
AND HE HAS BAD EXIDENT , BECAUSE HE ROLL-OFF.
CAR IS NEARLY COMPLITLY DESTROYED .  WE HAD BIG MEETING IN
FACTORY AND IT SEEMS TO US THAT IS IMPOSIBLE TO  PREPARE
IT READY BEFORE MONTE- CARLO START DAY .
WE ARE VERY SORRY. WE HOPE WILL MAKE COMPLYTLY NEW CAR FOR
YOU AND JUSSI FOR MARLBOLO ARTIC RALLY -76 SORRY THAT YOU CANT
START WITH POLSKI FIAT IN MONTE - CARLO THIS YEAR , BUT WE
CHECK OLL OUR POSSIBILITIES AND THERE IS NO CHANCE TO
REBUILT THAT CAR .

   EFESO WARSZAWA          POLSKI FIAT TEAM

   OBR
   Z- CA DYREKTORA  D/S KTORTKICH SREII
   /-/ INZ.  JOZEF KRAWCZAYNSKI



MAZMO TUN WELLS
814571 FSO PL
```

Some days you win . . .

Rallying full-time is the dream of many enthusiasts, but it is a dream that can only be enjoyed abroad. It is difficult to arrange a programme that involves more than fifty per cent of the time actually 'on the job'. This is because attractive events tend to coincide, and also because there are always a high proportion of arrangements that go wrong at the last minute, leaving the driver no time to make alternative plans. Let us say that an average rally lasts four days, including pre-rally scrutineering, and requires seven days' training. In addition to this time you will be spending another couple of days travelling to and from the event, while always there is a fair proportion of wasted time. This will arise through bad weather delaying flights or through delays in training with broken-down cars. Training is not, as you might expect, a system of physical jerks at seven in the morning; it is the essential business of driving round a rally route beforehand making plans for service and notes for use during the event. Although Britain has an excellent map network, and most events abroad supply route instructions designed to prevent your getting lost, only by actually seeing the obstacles on the route can you get a fair idea of the challenge of the event. This is quite apart from the work of making pace notes for the individual special stages, or for very tightly timed road sections.

Maps in foreign countries can be pretty deceptive. It is very difficult to tell how fast a stretch of road will be from looking at a map, and until you know how many minutes in hand you will have after a given section you will not know how long you will have for service – and until you have this information it is not possible to work out a service schedule for your mechanics. Although special stages are often repeated year after year, systems of note-making vary from driver to driver, and even from car to car for each driver. At best, having a set of notes from a previous year will only save one trip over a special stage. To do the job properly you still have to look at the stage afresh. Often there will be new road works, and there can also be dangerous fresh patches of gravel. When you see the terrain for yourself, you begin to understand the problems and can think about ways to overcome them. Training for rallies is both fascinating and frustrating. On the rallies themselves you go tearing through villages without ever having the chance to stop and study the places, and you pass the most glorious scenery in the dead of night. It is a chance to eat in local restaurants and stay in hotels miles away from civilization. It is also an opportunity to spend long boring hours waiting for people to come and rescue you after breakdowns!

The half-year spent at home is a far from idle period, as your telephone bill will soon testify. The degree to which you are involved with detailed team organization depends on the team concerned: obviously the smaller the team the more involved you will be. As a professional your first priority is to ensure that your plans work and that your team can rely implicitly upon your expertise, but rallying is still too small for attitudes that are inflexible. Your success is going to depend upon other people doing the right things, and if for no other reason than to protect yourself from things going wrong it is sensible to ensure that you work as closely with a team as they will want. Being self-dependent is, however, a prerequisite. Knowing how airline tickets work is a matter of self-preservation! If you are new to a team it is always difficult to know how much you are expected to help – and indeed whether the team would value the benefit of your previous experience.

Planning a series of rallies is far from easy: the further the rallies are

Training for rallies can be fascinating (Passo di Gouta, Italy)

Training can be frustrating! Silvio Maiga begins a long walk for help to rescue Munari's Lancia and Kynsilehto's Polski

from home, the more difficult the task becomes. The immediate problem which arises is whether it is best to team up permanently with one driver or simply to take offers of rides as and when they arise. Obviously the most successful co-drivers are those who are known for their allegiance to one driver in particular, but for every one successful driver/co-driver team there are dozens of co-drivers who have lost opportunities through staying with a driver too long. For reasons which are explained later I have never tied myself to one driver in particular, but this is not necessarily the best formula for others.

Reading regulations is a most important task, and is something to tackle as soon as they are published. However much various bodies have tried to standardize regulations they vary from event to event, and such is the nature of rallying that individual events demand individual rules. The bigger the rallies the more important it is to study the rules as early as possible, and the more involved the rules the more important it is for as many people as possible to study them and try to understand their full significance. A mastery over regulations is one of a professional's talents. Only when you have complete knowledge can you start to use the rules to your advantage.

One task that needs time when studying regulations for foreign rallies is comparison of the regulations with the copy in the official language. It is surprising how little knowledge of foreign languages you need in order to survive, though for rallying an ability to read French always helps. For the championship events abroad the official language is either French or English. It is always amusing to see little errors slip in. The Arctic Rally said that entries closed on 7th February – when the event took place the week before! The Ypres Rally had a very misleading clause about penalties for early and late arrival, and one word which always gives trouble is 'must', which can be confused with 'should'. Every mistake is a potential downfall – for you.

Whereas there are a considerable number of part-time co-drivers, full-time professional co-drivers are very few and far between. As a profession co-driving has little to commend itself; the future prospects are non-existent unless you have a special aptitude for management in which case one of the professional teams might wish to adopt you for this role in the future. Job security, even in the middle of a career, is negligible; whereas drivers derive a living out of a contract with a company, you will usually earn your fee from a driver, on an event-to-event basis. Contracts are double-edged affairs; whereas they ensure some security for payment of money, they are also an instrument for stopping you earning money, or even competing gratuitously, for another team. This lack of security means that unless a co-driver has another source of income a co-driving career is not attractive at all at the stage in his life when his talents are most useful. Obviously there are perks. Without doubt a place with a team is an élite position in the sport. You have well-prepared machinery (if not actually the best machinery!) and the enthusiasm of professional mechanics who are prepared to work extremely hard to enable you to succeed. When you

All cars will enter in par-fermé at the finish.

On 28/6/1975 cars come out of parc-fermé 1 h. before start-time. Re-start for second night as the established classification.

20. PENALITIES :

in less than target time : one minute	30 points
early than target time : one minute (lateness is non-cumulative).	60 points
per second late at a CH at the finish of a Chronometric Section	1 p.
per 1/10 second in exec of the fastest time on a Special Stage	1/10 p.

Exclusion : exceeding 30 min. lateness at CH in Ypres (end of lap) - Driving in the reserve direction on a Special-Stage — Use of a un registered car — Loss of/or alteration to Road-Book — Any fraud or unfair advantage — serious summons by Police.

21. RESULT :

This will be displayed in Hotel at 12 h. an will

Typical example of confusion due to translation. The reference to 'lateness' makes one assume that the word 'early' means 'after' . . .

d. Il n'est pas obligatoire de sortir la voiture du parc-fermé propulsée par son moteur.

e. Le Comité Organisateur décline toute responsabilité en ce qui concerne les véhicules abandonnés dans le parc-fermé, redevenu « voie publique » dès l'officialisation des résultats.

Art. 20. — RELEVE DES PENALITES

Pénalisations :

1. Routier :

   a. pour chaque minute ou fraction, en plus ou en moins des temps impartis, aux CH :
   par retatrd = 30 points
   par avance = 60 points.

   b. manque d'un visa à un CP. = 150 points.

2. a. Epreuves de classement :
   E.CHRON. : par seconde de retard = 1 point.
   E.S. par 1/10 de seconde = 1/10 point.
   (les temps réalisés sont comptabilisés en valeur réelle).

   b. plus de 3 min. entre le CH. et le Départ de l'E.S. = 30 points par minute.

3. Arrêt dans une Zone de Contrôle = 60 points.

. . . until you look at the French text, when you see that 'early' means 'early' and that 'in less than' means 'later than'. But which is correct? Somewhere else there should be a clause saying which text is right . . .

Rallye ou comme voitures « Officielles » et ne sont pas couverts par l'assurance du rallye. Elles restent sous la seule responsabilité du propriétaire.

Les conducteurs sont priés de faire lire attentivement les articles 6-7-10-18 par leurs équipes d'assistance.

e. Seuls les équipages constitués de deux conducteurs munis d'un Licence Internationale récolteront des points au Championnat d'Europe.

f. En cas de litige, seul le texte français fera foi.

g. La Firme BOSCH-ELDIS sera sur place avec service.

h. A tous les participants étrangers : gratuitement 3 nuits à l'hôtel + petit déjeuner.

i. Les résultats seront calculés et imprimés sur les machines I.B.M. gracieusement mis à la disposition des organisateurs par International Bussines Machines - I.B.M. Belgium.

. . . and in this case it is the French one

23

have found one position in a works team other positions are never quite so hard to find, and, of course, for two or three weeks at least you are spared that nagging worry about finding ways and means of making ends meet. Experience with professional teams certainly gives you a new outlook to your sport, a new care for detail and a new standard to emulate, quite apart from personal prestige.

Discomfort on the 1971 Scottish Rally

3 *So you want to be a rally driver?*
By CHRIS SCLATER

'How did you start rallying?' is probably the question I am asked most
frequently. I used to think of rally drivers as rather irresponsible
hooligans who made a point of waking me up every other Saturday
evening as they passed my home in Sussex. In fact my uncle, who
farmed not far away from us, actually confronted a rally car with a
12-bore shotgun after it had taken a wrong turning and finished up
stuck in his cattle-yard.

In the days when I was at college in Brighton we had a motor club
mainly interested in motor racing. Amongst the members was Peter
McDowell who happened to be Sydney Allard's nephew. Peter was
rallying one of Sydney's old Anglias and persuaded me to marshal on a
local club rally that Saturday evening. I co-opted a friend to navigate
me in my Mini-van. Having attended the marshals' meeting, off we
went to our appointed position somewhere on Salisbury Plain. Getting
to our remote map reference was a rally in itself. When we were in
position the whole business became fascinating. We watched the sky
being lit up by the spotlights of the rally cars minutes before they
appeared. We did not know where they were coming from and, after we
had given them a card, we did not know where they were going as they
disappeared out of sight. My opinion of rallying was changing.

I joined a local car club and became involved in the activities that car
clubs put on, even helping to organize a driving-test meeting and a
small rally. The motor clubs of the country are the life-blood of motor
sport and in particular of rallying, which is the most popular. Through
the motor clubs I met navigators and people who were keen to be
involved with car preparation and assisting generally. I marshalled a
few more times and then had the chance to buy an Anglia which,
although rotten with rust, had – amazingly – a Weber carburettor, a
sumpshield and some spotlights. It cost £50. Every evening was spent
working on the car. Every penny and more was spent on it; and in
October 1966 I entered my first rally. It was the Sussex Car Club's
Olympic, and we finished – twenty-fourth.

I don't remember a great deal about the first event except that I
thoroughly enjoyed it and was completely worn out when we reached
the finish at some seedy café on the A23. I do remember that it had two
selective sections, one of which was on Pevensey Marshes. Selectives
in those days were used, as the name suggests, as tie deciders only. The
average speed we had to attain seemed very high although that didn't
seem to worry too many people!

Early days with the GT Anglia (Bristowe Rally)

I entered two more road rallies of the same type and then came the Dursley Car Club's event in South Wales. This was a mixture of special stages and selectives. Although I had to retire before the end (the exhaust broke and started to gas us), I realized that this was a part of the sport I would find very difficult to give up. The sheer excitement that came from driving a car quickly over loose surfaces with the incredible noise of stones rattling against the floor and the feeling of the car sliding from corner to corner, was fantastic.

Wales also opened up a completely new idea of rallying. This was real rally country with countless mountain roads and not a policeman for miles. The problem was that it took several hours to drive there (with an inevitable extra cost in petrol) but I decided that I would try to do as many Welsh rallies as possible. Things didn't quite turn out like that though. Progress was quicker than I thought.

After one more road rally the Anglia was sold to some luckless soul and another one bought – this time with a 1500 GT engine. This was living. Disc brakes, wide wheels, a roof light and ... heavier insurance.

I decided to enter a bigger event with some 'names' in the entry and see how well I could do. Having been bitten by the sport I didn't want to sink my entire earnings into it and still be a third-rate driver, so I chose to enter the Isle of Wight Rally. My navigator for these early events was Peter Moss, an old school-friend – also converted from the motor racing spectators' club. The 1967 Isle of Wight Rally was all special stages and from the little I remember some were better than others. It was very wet and very muddy but there were one or two good forests. The result I know (mine anyway) – ninth. This was my eighth rally. One more stage rally in 1967, the Safari South Wales, gave me my best result, fifth.

Studies in mechanical engineering at college were beginning to suffer. Time was being spent working on the car when it should have been spent working on books, and I was facing a dilemma. Should I carry on with rallying purely and simply as a hobby and sport, or should I get involved in the sporting side of the motor trade and use it to help my rallying as well as to earn a living?

I decided on the latter. I gave up mechanical engineering studies and went to work in London for the Allard Motor Company under Alan Allard, who was Sydney Allard's son. I was put in charge of the shop, selling goodies mainly for Fords, and spent most of my time on the phone arranging my rallying activities. It was about this time that the ban on advertising on competition cars was lifted. This was a real help. I persuaded Alan to support my entries by paying the entry fees and petrol expenses in return for advertising the company on the car and for acting as company spokesman on rallies.

Toward the middle of 1968 the idea of driving in the Gulf London International came into my mind. If I was going to enter an international, this was the one. Gulf were providing free petrol and as the longest, toughest international in the British calendar the Gulf would give best value for the entry fee, which I think was about £30. The only problem was a car. The Anglia wasn't really up to it and anyway didn't comply with the regulations. To my rescue came Peter McDowell. He was still at college in Brighton and couldn't take part in the rally because he had examinations right up to the day of the start. So he very generously lent me his Lotus Cortina on condition that I put it back into good condition after the rally.

Collar and tie in those days (Gulf, London, 1968)

I sold the Anglia for a small profit and, with a couple of weeks to go, began to prepare the Cortina. In fact there wasn't much preparation to do because although the car was almost standard apart from the sump-guard, high ratio steering box and stiffer shock absorbers, I hadn't actually any spare money to put into it.

The next problem was a co-driver. I decided that I should take somebody more experienced than myself so that the world of international rallies wouldn't be a complete mystery to both of us. I had heard about Martin Holmes and had watched him at a distance on road rallies; I had even heard that drivers had to pay for his services! Nevertheless I decided that he was the first choice. I plucked up courage one evening to phone him – and he actually agreed to go with me. He did mention in passing that his wife was due to have a baby two weeks after the rally, but didn't think that would be a problem.

So – off we went to the Gulf. For the first time I had a service car. The crew were Peter Moss and Peter McDowell who joined at the last minute. The 'service car' was Moss's father's Triumph 2000 Estate car, which incidentally was quicker than the rally car but never the same afterwards! We had no spares for the rally car apart from four wheels and tyres and a fanbelt. Most of the Triumph was occupied by a pair of full-size welding bottles, food, a few tools and a jack.

The other attraction of the Gulf was that it was virtually non-stop for four days and three nights, so there was no need for the expense of hotels – which I couldn't have afforded anyway. Martin gave me strict instructions to take it easy and see how we were doing at half-way. After the second stage he got quite angry: 'If you drive at that speed we won't get further than the next stage . . . but I did enjoy it.' So did I.

Just before half-way at Manchester, where we were due to have all of three hours' sleep, I stuck the car head-first off the road and into a tree.

We got back on to the road with the help of some spectators and another competitor. The radiator was bent like a banana and empty of water, but luckily it was down hill off the stage. We made a temporary repair and stayed in the rally. The only other problem was a broken throttle linkage – which happened just as we crossed the finishing line of a stage. How lucky can you get? Otherwise the car ran perfectly and we were ninth overall and winner of our class.

I was too shy to stay for the prize-giving and anyway had to be back at work. The whole event had cost nothing at all, although the car was so tired I had to buy it from Peter. But it was worth it just to have a result like that on my first international rally. I was on cloud nine for weeks. (Incidentally, Martin's wife produced a son on the third day of the rally.)

At this point it was clear that I was well and truly involved in rallying. I had made a start and a fairly successful one. I had taken a few steps up the ladder missing out some of the rungs, but it had worked out. I was certainly lucky, luckier than most people, but success in a sport which is as expensive as rallying relies to a large extent on luck as well as determination.

It is possible, however, to test your ability, to get involved and to enjoy yourself without having to spend a lot of money. The motor trade background is obviously a tremendous advantage. But interest in the mechanical side of the motor car and a practical ability will help tremendously with cost-savings. When it comes to entering a rally there will be times when mechanical ability will get you to the finish, and even help you win an event. I remember the Circuit of Ireland Rally in 1970 when Roger Clark was driving a Group 6 (Prototype) Escort with a racing-type rear suspension. An important bolt broke on a link locating the back axle. He was leading the rally and it was impossible to get to the service crew in time. Roger found a bolt on another part of the car and used it to fix the axle. The job itself wasn't very easy for a mechanic, and Roger had probably never worked on that axle before. But he fixed it, stayed in the rally, and won. His background in the motor trade had paid off.

If you want to be involved in rallying for little expense, then navigating or marshalling is the answer. If you enjoy it, then move on and try your hand at driving. If it doesn't appeal to you, then it has cost you very little. Certainly, if you do want to become involved, your spare time will be fully occupied. You must be prepared for this – and make sure other members of your family are as well. They can be kept occupied with the administration side of the team, keeping in touch with local interest, press and local radio, for instance.

When you reach the level of championship special stage rallying there are several ways to learn and improve. Go to spectate on the national and international rallies. Learn from the professionals. Look at the equipment they use and the ideas that go into the cars and the preparation for an event. You will never beat the works teams but you can benefit from the testing and development that they pay for. Look at the equipment they use – tyres, lights, seats and so on. You may not be able to afford equipment at this level but you can probably use the next best – or adapt and improvise for yourself. By being around at the big events you will be more likely to be in the right place at the right time. Believe me, this is the most important factor towards success.

A visit to a rally school is very worth while. As I will describe in a later chapter, it is possible to learn very quickly sitting beside an expert driver, and a session at the Ford Rally School will give you plenty of practical experience in both seats of a rally car. If you have natural ability the school will bring it out and improve it.

If, after all this, you still have the money and enthusiasm to con-

No. 86

MARTIN HOLMES

ONE 6lb boy
ARRIVED ON TIME

NO EXTRA PENALTY

David Sengh

CLERK OF THE COURSE

Special announcement on the Gulf

If you have an accident make it a big one! . . .
Then try to use it to advantage (1969 Scottish Rally)

tinue, and to continue up the scale, then give yourself a time limit for
the various steps. Don't try to run before you can walk, though. Two
years to get a national licence, and a further year for an international, is
quite quick enough. Of course, people have entered international
rallies in the first year of competition, but rallying is a sport where
above all experience pays off handsomely with the results.

My philosophy in the early days was always to try hard and never to be frightened of asking. The turning point in my career was the Scottish Rally in 1969. I was driving a Lotus Cortina, in fact the same car I had driven to second place on the Welsh earlier in the year. I was full of confidence; too much confidence, clearly, because on stage 28 – Ardgartan – I flew (literally) off the road and fifty feet down a vertical drop. But I was leading the rally at the time, and this was important. I had been 'noticed', although I didn't realize it at the time.

When I eventually got home with the wreckage, I telephoned Stuart Turner, who was then Ford's Competition Manager, and before I could say much, he said: 'Oh good, we want to see you, when can you come over?' The result was a works Escort at a very reasonable price and the promise of assistance to run it. This was incredible – out of a disaster had come the biggest boost I could ever wish for. But only because of my philosophy of driving hard from the start. Retiring when lying nowhere proves nothing about your ability. This attitude has to change once you are established, although the plain fact that first past the post is the winner still remains.

A classic example of this sort of story is Ari Vatanen, who became a works driver for Ford at the age of twenty-three. His early rallying in Finland was in a rather tatty, fairly reliable Opel Ascona. He always drove flat out from the start – and either crashed or did extremely well. On occasions he beat Timo Makinen himself. The result was a one-off drive for Ford in the Thousand Lakes Rally, Finland's premier event. He led for seven stages and then crashed. Ford still had faith in him and he drove for them on the RAC Rally the same year. He drove very sensibly in the early stages but was caught out by a bad jump and destroyed the car. But his times had established him as a driver of tremendous potential. The result was a permanent drive for Ford and an obviously rosy future. The ability to fight back after set-backs is a quality that team managers and sponsors look for.

Never give up! Pressing on after a minor disaster (1970 Scottish Rally)

4 *Beginnings for a co-driver*
By MARTIN HOLMES

First rally for Martin was in this old Triumph. The ford looked so deep he got out of the car first!

I still recall my amazement when a friend returned to our digs, looking as if he had not slept for the past forty-eight hours, and announced without any sign of surprise that he hadn't. He had always had an odd, far-away look which gave him an air of mystery. Where had he been? What had gone wrong? He had been to Wales, he thought he had said that before he went, and they had left the road on a rally. A crash? Was anyone hurt? Nothing unusual, it seemed. The real cause for concern was that they had been doing so well at the time. What an adventure! It was to me an irresistible challenge. I joined the local motor club to find out about the sport of competing in cars, something an impecunious amateur could enjoy. It was three years before I was able to go to Wales to compete on a rally, but those three years were spent enjoying all the local events, little treasure hunts and even some of the big restricted events which attracted competitors from over a hundred miles away. To me those three years were the best grounding anyone could have had for learning the job of rally co-driving. This was quite a long time ago. Now there is a much wider choice. Where should you begin?

What kind of event?

The first decision is whether to dive in at the deep end as soon as you can or whether to learn things gradually. Co-drivers and drivers differ in their demands. Little events teach drivers a lot of bad techniques, whereas they train co-drivers in a positive way. Co-drivers provide the fund of experience within a rally car and little local events provide the quickest way of gaining experience cheaply and quickly. On every rally you learn things that you can carry forward for the next occasion. Until fairly recently you could enter a world championship event without any previous experience at all. The trouble with this sort of thing is that you can ruin an event through a simple misunderstanding of the sport, or through ignorance of something you could have learned harmlessly and inexpensively competing only a few miles away from home. Furthermore, on local events you learn all the principles without the complications of mechanical unreliability or of sophisticated equipment. In the old days I used to compete using parking lights for map-reading, and for the first event I ever entered we used torches for map-reading at night. The first time we entered a restricted status event we were nearly thrown out of scrutineering. We did not have a reversing lamp warning light. One hundred cars before us had a warning light; it was required by law. Why didn't we have one? We couldn't afford a reversing lamp! We still won the novice prize, though I concede we did get lost once or twice.

What must you know?

What knowledge does a co-driver need if he is to have a future in the sport? He needs an indefinable feel for the sport. This is largely understanding how an organizer would view a situation. To this extent it is very good training for any co-driver to organize an event himself from time to time. It used to be said that you could guarantee a future event would be enjoyable if you knew the name of the organizer as a competitor, and only the full-time professionalism required for organizing the major events has done anything to alter the truth of this saying. For a competitor to have organizing experience is the converse. You can judge with confidence which of two steps you should take, or maybe decide not to pursue a course of action which might lead to unexpected trouble. On small events this sort of instinct might persuade you to prejudge the likely route an event will take, on bigger events you might well prejudge whether or not your proposed servicing locations will lead to dispute with marshals. On a different tack altogether, as an organizer you know the sort of logic that would persuade you to cancel penalties on a section, and the sort of logic that would harden you against such action. Not everything you will glean on these small events will be of ultimate benefit to you, but it will help you progress to the next step in your sporting career.

It is important to enter as many rallies as you can, not only because this increases your fund of knowledge but also because you meet and know more people. Furthermore, the more you go rallying the less you

Only experience will tell you if an organizer will cancel the timing on a stage in circumstances like this. Colin Malkin, Shekhar Mehta and Colin Grewer ponder their next step

suffer from the pressure of the moment. This kind of pressure is something you rarely suffer in ordinary life, perhaps except before and during an important examination. If you read a set of route instructions in the peace of your home you will have no trouble in correctly interpreting what they say; but if you read the same set in a rally car, knowing that time is running against you and under the motion of a moving car, your understanding will be far less complete. Somehow the normal human brain has a tendency to stop functioning in such circumstances, and experience is the best way to train it to work properly. Small treasure hunts are an almost unrivalled way to gain this kind of experience.

How fast should you progress?

In Britain we have a system of upgrading of licences, which in basic terms means that we cannot jump in at the deep end of rallying too quickly. We have to gain experience at lower levels before going too far upward. It is still experience that we can gain pretty fast, so you must soon decide how quickly to progress. I spent a long time competing on road rallies. This was largely because I had a nine-to-five existence, and stage rallies then were major events, all of which required time off work. The one-day stage events came later. I am convinced that the road rallies in the late 'sixties and early 'seventies were a far better training-ground for co-drivers than they were ever given credit for. Even in the mid-seventies Ford were still tending to choose co-drivers who had made their mark in road rallying even though road rallying as a training-ground for drivers had been dismissed years previously. So where should you go when you have done a few small club rallies and decided that you enjoy competition in cars? This depends on how much you like road rallying, and how much you prefer events with

stages.

Road rallies were good training grounds for co-drivers. Martin seen here winning his first Motoring News *championship event – the Illuminations – with Paul Faulkner*

Working under flat-out conditions (Richard Iliffe, Ford Escort RS 1600)

Working at four in the morning (Martin with Russell Brookes)

Road rallies

Road rallying is progressively being slowed down. The roads of Britain, because of the overall speed limits and the increasing number of cars on the road, are now no longer the place for competitive sport with powerful cars. If you want to make your name as a leading co-driver you must turn to stage events, because only on these events can you experience the pleasure and learn the art of working under the conditions of being driven flat out. This is probably a pity because road rallying can teach you many other attributes, not the least of which is working when you are tired. It takes a special skill to make logical and correct decisions when you are also busy directing your driver through the lanes – at four o'clock in the morning. You can develop in road rallying an automation of navigation when you are tired, a sense which enables you to think about other problems yet still correctly read the maps and think about time-keeping. This sort of attribute is essential for foreign rallying, when you have pace notes to read during a stage in addition to thinking about the general management of the rally car – and you are working long hours as well. In the next few years it is obvious that the British factory rally teams are going to have to choose co-drivers who have been brought up within this road rally experience, **35**

John Brown map-reading during the 1975 Circuit of Ireland with Russell Brookes

and it is going to be very interesting to see if they will have the same success as people like Henry Liddon, Jim Porter and John Davenport who cut their rallying teeth on the public roads in the middle of the night.

Road rallying trains co-drivers in many ways. It develops a special curiosity about maps and map reading – and an enjoyment of reading maps is an essential for successful co-driving. Different maps tell you different things, and certainly the Michelin maps in France tell you completely different details from those given on the British Ordnance Survey sheets. What you must have is the desire to learn from maps, to rely on your interpretation of maps, and to anticipate how maps can be deficient in various respects. Although it is probably wrong that stage rallying should demand competence in map-reading for a good result, it is a pity that young stage rally co-drivers do not have the opportunity to develop this skill. I do not think in my time there has ever been a better map-reader than John Brown. I once co-drove Richard Martin-Hurst on a *Motoring News* event. John's driver never appeared at the start, and out of a fit of lunacy Richard and I agreed to take John as a passenger in the back, on condition that he sat there, said nothing and simply helped to lift the car back on the road should we have an accident. To me it was an incredible experience. I was navigating in my usual manner, and John would correct me or give suggestions. Most of the suggestions came as interpretations of the maps. Things went absolutely perfectly until we came to a fork. John yelled 'left', I shouted 'right' – and Richard went straight on and missed the junction altogether. Careful description about where to turn for junctions can save minutes lost in hesitation.

When Russell Brookes and John finished fifth on the 1975 Circuit of Ireland Rally, in a Group 1 RS2000, I asked him how he was able to go so fast on various stages, and he explained that John was able to read the road from the maps. If you study Irish half-inch maps you will see that they do not have anything like the accuracy of the British maps, although the bad corners are generally marked, and marked in the right places. John used his years of experience from British road rallying to remarkable effect. For an accomplished stage rally driver you need really proficient map-reading to speed a driver up at all; to speed such a driver up on the minor Irish roads was an extraordinary achievement. I was able to read these Irish maps usefully on the '76 'Circuit' when my driver Pat Ryan had serious brake trouble. Foreknowledge of impending sharp corners made our progress much safer.

Stage events

Road rallying these days gives a one-sided view of the sport. Very many more people are starting rallying on stage events, and it is almost inevitable that this trend will continue. In the same way that road rallying is not a full training-ground for the major events, so the ordinary club stage event cannot provide all the training you need. The benefit of a club stage rally background is that you discover early on whether you enjoy being driven flat-out or not. (You never have this experience on road events.) You have all the training in general management you can want: the experience of arranging entries, of handling service crews, of dealing with marshals. But there are drawbacks. You need not show any particular flair in order to succeed. Before any road rally driver will win, he has to be directed around the route faultlessly by his navigator, and that is a skill few can manage. Your flair in stage rallying is usually only called upon if there is trouble. A stage rally co-driver is seldom responsible for a driver winning a rally; in road rallying he usually is! Because of this distinction, co-drivers often gain rides for the wrong reasons. Maybe they find sponsorship, maybe they are handy with the tools. There is little opportunity to develop the positive aspects of the job on these events.

Reading pace notes

At least a co-driver can gain experience of map-reading if he is inclined to go in for road rallies, but experience of pace note reading is something that cannot be properly learned except by rallying consistently abroad. In Britain the only rallies on which pace notes are allowed are the Manx Trophy Rally run in the United Kingdom and Donegal in Eire. Previously pace notes had been allowed on other events unless banned, but since the beginning of 1976 they have been banned on stage rallies in Britain unless specifically permitted. The only places where pace notes can now be permitted generally are on road rallies – rallies where the open roads will stop a driver from going at full speed anyway. Driving over loose-surfaced roads never benefits from pace notes to quite the same degree as driving over asphalt roads. The forest roads in particular have a habit of changing surface over the months, and of changing width as well. In addition, rally cars built for forest driving are designed for the driver to deal with unexpected situations,

Achim Warmbold winning the 1975 Donegal Rally

Billy Coleman is a secret route driver. Martin co-drives him on the 1974 Dukeries Rally.

whereas pace notes are designed to enable the driver to drive smoothly knowing that unexpected situations will not occur. Even the Isle of Man or Donegal Rallies cannot provide a very good grounding for learning to make pace notes, even if the opportunity for learning were sufficient. The stages are short and consequently are easily memorized, so that a driver will never put his real trust in the notes. He will simply use them to back up his own particular memory. Of particular interest here was the way Achim Warmbold won the 1975 Donegal Rally. Achim is a pace note driver first and foremost. He had never been to Ireland before, and only gave himself time before the event to drive over each stage twice. He relied on his notes to such good effect that he won the rally outright, beating all the successful local men. By way of comparison, Billy Coleman went to Spain with John Davenport (the same co-driver that Warmbold had used in Donegal) for the Firestone Rally earlier in the year. Billy is a secret route driver, and although he and John made good notes so that he had a good safe rally to second place, he was beaten – by a quarter of an hour – by a real pace note expert, Verini, who drove a Fiat Abarth with considerably less power. You need a lot of experience in pace notes for them to be really effective.

You never stop learning in rallying because the challenge is always taking fresh turnings. The essentials for a co-driver are that he never fails to remember a lesson when one is learned – by him or anyone else – and that he never misses an opportunity to learn. This is why I think it is important not to confine yourself to one driver. It is true that some of the greatest teams in rallying have been people who only rally with each other, but even in these cases the people concerned originally started their careers in different directions. Drivers and co-drivers have different careers; the only reason why they have to consider each other is that they need each other. For a driver, success will only come if he has a co-driver in whom he can place his trust and confidence; for a co-driver success will only come with a driver fast enough to win. Each uses the other in pursuit of his own career! This of course does not stop some very profitable partnerships being formed, or some strong preferences when it comes to choosing which rallies to enter or which drivers to compete with. It is not loyalty for a co-driver to miss opportunities to enter other rallies if his regular driver cannot compete. What will happen on those occasions in the future when they can compete together again? Will the driver thank the co-driver for being ignorant of a dodgy bend which he could have known about had he entered another event with someone else? On every event you enter, you have the chance to meet fresh people. Rallying fortunately is too friendly a sport for you to know people just for what you can get out of them in the future, but the element that the people you meet might one day be able to help you still remains. And the person who will benefit most from your acquaintances is the driver you are worried about leaving behind at home.

Rallying is too expensive to be an ordinary sport. It is a sport where a lot of money, and consequently a lot of satisfaction, can be thrown away through inexperience. The co-driver can bring the knowledge and experience to a driver. It is essential for you to rally as often as you can, and also not to enter events too willingly when you are not able to offer much experience. One of the best ways to learn about events without costing someone else disappointment or expense is simply to go and watch, maybe to assist the service crew of some other driver. In this way you will be able to go to a rally without much expense and learn things which you can never do simply by reading the magazines the week after. Maybe you will even see other people make the sort of mistakes you might have made. Even if you do not know one end of a spanner from another, you will still be appreciated as a map-reader. The presence of a competent navigator in a service car is a real luxury for a driver, if only because he knows that he can expect to see his mechanics in places which otherwise might be too remote for them to find.

Understeer

5 *Is sideways safest?*
By CHRIS SCLATER

In 1971, when Ford were experiencing problems with halfshaft failure on the Escort, I was involved with driving a car for hours on end round the test track at Bagshot to try to break halfshafts. The idea was to find the type of shaft which lasted longest. Roger Clark was also driving and we would alternate – five laps each until a shaft broke, then try another one, and so on. When Roger drove I sat with him, and from watching him I learnt more about technique than I would have done in dozens of rallies. Occasionally he would sit with me and comment on my bad points and, sometimes, good points!

It's impossible to force ability on to someone. Ability must be there in the first place, but technique can be taught to supplement that ability. That is what I learnt from Roger – just sitting in the same car was improving my own driving. In this chapter I will explain the problems and natural hazards found in all the different types of rallying, and the ways to cope with them.

As far as the driver is concerned, rallies fall into two basic categories: those whose competitive route is announced in advance permitting crews either to practise at speed or at least to look over the roads, and those whose route is kept secret until the crews drive over it on the rally. When I say the competitive part, I mean the special stages. The liaison sections on the RAC Rally for instance are announced a week in advance and the RAC Rally is accepted as a secret route rally. Most British special stage rallies are of the secret type and most of the stages are on loose-surfaced forest roads. So let us consider the driving techniques for those events first.

Driving on loose-surfaced roads

Beating the understeer

The coefficient of friction between tyre and road is lower on gravel than on tarmac. In other words there is less grip. An obvious fact, but still very important to establish. If you drive on these roads in a conventional way you have to drive very slowly round the corners or you will slide off the road. This is mainly because of 'understeer'.

In simple terms understeer is when the car doesn't follow the instruction you give it with the steering wheel, but slides toward the outside of the corner, front first. Understeer also occurs on tarmac but

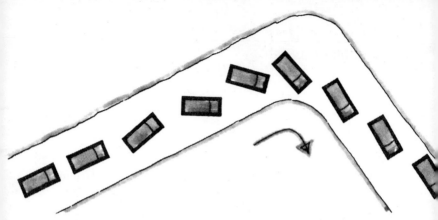

to a far lesser extent. Suspension can be modified to reduce the effect on loose surfaces but car specifications have to be a compromise because of the variety of conditions which are faced. If you eliminated understeer on gravel, the car would be undriveable on tarmac, so you must adapt your driving style to beat the understeer on loose surfaces. Once you have done this, fast special stage times are within your reach.

Assume that the car you are driving is of conventional layout – that is front-engined, rear-wheel drive – and you are approaching a fairly sharp right-hand corner. Position the car in the middle of the road and force it into an unstable condition by turning the wheel sharply to the left. By closing the throttle and overcorrecting the skid you have induced, you will swing the car back across your direction of travel so that you are now beating the understeer and are in a position to drive round the corner in a slide, balance the car with the throttle, and steer toward the inside of the corner against the momentum (or centrifugal force) which is trying to take you toward the outside of the corner and off the road. It is vital to your speed through the corner and up the next straight that you don't allow the car to go further sideways than necessary.

Hazards

Corners The position of the car as it goes round a corner depends on the natural hazards – rocks, ditches or banks for example – but in general try to straighten the bend as soon as possible. This not only makes you faster but gives maximum visibility. If visibility is limited, take an early apex. By doing this you are in the safest position if the corner turns out to be tighter than you thought. It may seem odd that instability is safest, but this is a fact. A car can be made to stop very quickly if travelling sideways because stones build up in front of the tyres. In addition, direction can be changed drastically and suddenly. Read the road all the way round the corner. Humps and bumps will throw your car off the optimum line very quickly and you must immediately correct the changes of direction with the steering. Slow reactions on the steering and not enough movement are the faults that everybody shows at rally schools. Remember that rallies are won by seconds nowadays.

That then is the principle behind fast cornering on loose surfaces, particularly when the road is unfamiliar. Now let's look in more detail at the range of corners and the best and safest way to get round them.

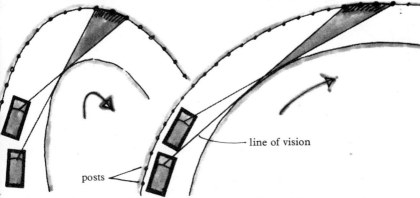

line of vision

posts

Judging the degree of a corner before you reach it or while you are in it is obviously very desirable. I have a way of doing this which only pays off on fast roads although it adds to safety on slower ones. Consider a corner with a series of equidistant posts or a fence round the outside. The quicker the next post becomes visible the faster is the corner. The longer it takes before you see the next post, the slower it is. Naturally not many stages have fences along their entire length but the principle is there, and with practice it can be adapted to apply to the natural scenery of any road.

Before a corner or any other hazard you must be in a position to stop the car within your vision. A crest could hide a very nasty corner, or equally a very easy one. Either way your reactions must be very fast whether you are going back on the throttle or coping with the problems of negotiating the hazard.

Once you have slowed the car for the next corner and have made a judgement on its severity you must concentrate on passing round it in the most economical way. Concentrate on leaving at the highest possible speed in the right direction, i.e. pointing up the straight to the next hazard.

Most cars steer very well on slight corners and these can be taken either on a neutral line or with a slight oversteering, the oversteer in this case being initiated by the throttle. Hold the car in a true slide with the tail held slightly out and the power on. In this way, if the corner tightens up on you, it is possible to let the tail go a bit further by either backing off (closing the throttle) or opening the throttle fully and at the same time steering into the bend. Which method you use depends on road conditions, but try to keep power on as much as possible for maximum safety. With wheels spinning the car is very unlikely to **43**

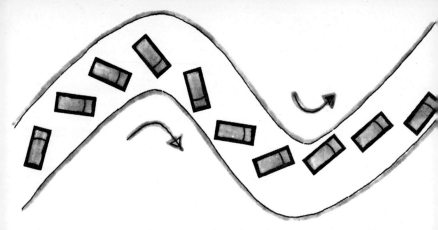

catch in a rut and turn over, since there is no resistance to sideways motion.

As corners become sharper and sharper so it becomes more and more important to put the car into an unbalanced condition. This can be hard work and sometimes you'll have to be very vicious with the car, but it is vital for fast times. If you have spectated on rallies like the RAC Rally you will understand what I mean. The cars are sometimes 'thrown' very violently out of line to get the swinging motion started in order to beat the understeer.

In an S bend or series of sharp corners, the swing of the car can be used to set you up for the following corner. Knowing that a sharp left-hand corner is following a sharp right-hand one, let the tail go a bit wide on the exit to the right. Then by backing off and overcorrecting with the steering, the car will swing back across the direction of travel to enable you to put on the power and oversteer round the left-hander.

The tightest corner you meet is a hairpin. Although every driver treats a hairpin in a different way there is a standard technique which has to be modified because of the many variations of this type of corner. Approach the bend on the inside, i.e. on the right side for a right-hand corner. Force the car into an unbalanced condition under braking by steering to the left, back off and steer to the right, so swinging across the axis. This time let it go much further so that the car is right across the road with the inside wheel absolutely on the apex of the bend. By using the power, the tail of the car should describe an arc about the right-hand front wheel, which will be almost stationary, until you are pointing up the straight on the exit of the corner.

Sometimes hairpins are extremely tight and narrow in which case the handbrake has to be used. Skill with the handbrake is a very useful asset as it can help you out of panic situations as well as get you round difficult hairpins. If you lock up the rear brakes only and therefore cause loss of adhesion between road and rear wheels, there is no resistance to sideways movement of the back of the car while the front wheels are still gripping and steering. With a conventional layout car you must use the clutch to disconnect the drive train at the same time as you pull the handbrake on very hard. Because you have pressed the

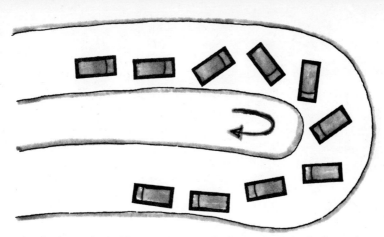

clutch, the engine will not stall when the rear wheels lock. Once the handbrake has done its job (without losing the steering) and the car is sliding, let it off and at the same time let the clutch in and open the throttle. The slide will then continue and you can balance the car smoothly round the corner with throttle and steering.

Blind crests   Never approach a blind crest in a straight line. As you brake for the crest put the car out of line. This has two advantages. First, it means that your four wheels are all making their own tracks in the road and are therefore giving better retardation. Second and more important, you are in a position to deal with whatever is beyond the crest. For instance: you are approaching a crest and beyond is a T-junction, but you don't see the arrow until you are over the crest. Put the car a little sideways with the tail hung to the right. If the road goes left all you need do is use the throttle to increase the angle of the car and slide round the corner. If it goes right, then you are already in the unbalanced situation and can easily 'swing' the other way by backing off and overcorrecting, which will put you in a position to negotiate the corner smoothly and safely.

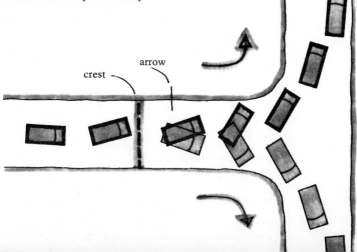

crest

arrow

Good positioning and attitude for a tight left-hander. (Portugal, 1974).

Too much sideways loses time. The big Datsun 240 Z causing problems (Chris and Martin, 1974 Welsh Rally)

Bridges and gates   Another hazard that occurs frequently is the small bridge over a stream with about a six-inch high concrete parapet on each side. This can be an extremely dangerous hazard, because if you catch the parapet with a wheel you can easily bend the axle or even knock off a wheel. Normally an advance hazard warning is given, but not always. Either way it is important to line up the car in good time because the concrete or wooden surface of the bridge will always be slippery. A similar technique should be applied to gateways. The posts can narrow the track down to as little as eight feet in some places and the area near the gate is more slippery because of traffic that stops and starts to open the gate in normal use.

Fire-breaks   Probably the worst hazard encountered by rally drivers in the forests is the fire-break. To reduce the chances of a forest fire spreading, strips of the forest are kept clear of trees and where convenient these clearances coincide with the forest roads. However, sometimes this is not convenient, and where the road takes a sharp turn the fire-break may continue straight on.

When you are driving at speed you concentrate on that part of the road which is perhaps two seconds' driving time ahead of you, and at seventy miles an hour this is about seventy yards. It is easy to get lulled into following the line of trees down a straight and then find that suddenly, over a slight crest, the road goes sharp right – and there you are doing seventy, still following that break in the trees, and no chance of getting round the corner.

The best drivers regularly get caught out by the fire-break corners. There is no technique to deal with them except vigilance. There are certain areas where they occur frequently, and all I can suggest is that you should be on your guard the whole time and try to make a note of the stages in case you use them on another rally.

Driving on tarmac

Tyres

Driving on tarmac is a different story. First, you must have the right tyres for the job. Nowadays most people use racing tyres, although their high cost forces many to stick to radial tyres, or to radial racers which are radial tyres fitted with a racing pattern.

Racing tyres give incredible adhesion between tyre and road and for this reason it is very difficult to make the car slide – and in fact unnecessary. Another point is that when a car fitted with racing tyres starts to slide, the breakaway is so sudden that you can lose control very easily and very quickly.

I remember the first time I used racers I didn't like the feeling at all. I was trying to throw the car about and make it slide on the road as it would have done with radials. As soon as I drove more like a racing driver – getting the braking over before the corner and concentrating on using all the road to take the easiest, smoothest line – I began to go   47 considerably faster, and was a lot happier as well. Driving a car with all that grip takes it out on your arm and shoulder muscles, though. I remember on the Monte in 1973, after completing a very twisty forty-five-kilometre special stage, I could hardly grip the wheel because the tendons on the inside of my wrist were aching so much.

When you are driving on unknown roads on racing tyres, there will be occasions when you need to unbalance the car to cope with the unpredictable. I certainly wouldn't recommend inducing a slide, but by being a bit brutal you can transfer weight either from back to front or side to side to help the situation.

Pace Notes

Nearly every continental rally except for those in Sweden and Finland can be practised. The route is published well in advance. Most of the stages are on public roads which are closed to everything except the rally. In order to close the roads the closing orders have to be announced a month or so before the event so even if the organizers didn't publish the route it wouldn't take long for competitors to find it out for themselves. The result is a different type of rally driver and a different sort of rally. Pace notes are used on all but the smallest, and because of this reliance on notes few continental drivers can compete favourably on secret-route rallies. The Swedes and Finns are the exception because the majority of their events are secret. (The Thousand Lakes Rally in Finland, however, is not.)

The situation with British drivers is the opposite. Like the Swedes and Finns we drive on unknown roads for ninety per cent of the rallies; for one event – the Manx Rally – the route is published. The result of this situation is that pace notes are a bit of a mystery to most British drivers, and they find that driving on known roads requires different techniques from the ones they are used to.

The principles of pace note driving apply equally to tarmac and loose surfaces. Making pace notes and putting them into practice successfully is not easy. Using pace notes is a way to help you drive quickly that takes years to perfect, requires extreme concentration – but can be very satisfying. Arguments about pace notes go on for hours among drivers and co-drivers, but in the end it's up to the individual to make the best of whichever system he chooses.

My first experience with pace notes was on the *Coupe des Alpes* in 1969. I did the rally in an Escort with the Welsh co-driver Hywel Thomas. Because we only had a few days to recce I borrowed a set of notes from Ove Andersson and John Davenport who were driving in the Ford team. Despite being Swedish, Ove makes notes in English and in a system which John had used with Vic Elford and others. Knowing that these notes had been tested at rally speeds we knew they were accurate. In this way I could learn how to use a well-tried system and next time I would be in a position to make notes in this system for myself. I did, and have used a variation on that system ever since. I wouldn't say that my system of notes is perfect, but it works for me.

In any system, pace notes are written as an abbreviation of words that describe the road and the direction of the corners. The important point is that they describe the road and not the speed of the car, so that no matter how the conditions change the notes still mean the same thing. There are eight basic corners described in reducing order of speed:

Flat Left – Ĺ
Slight Left – SL
Fast Left – FL
Fast K Left – FKL
K Left – KL
Left – L
Open Hairpin Left – OHPL
Hairpin Left – HPL

As important as the corners are the ways in which they are connected. This may be either a short straight of, say, fifty metres, a long straight of up to six hundred metres, or there may well be no straight at all between two corners. Whatever the distance is, it must be made clear in the notes, because it is vital for the driver to know this distance as it affects how he accelerates out of the previous corner. In my notes, a short straight of less than fifty metres is 'and' written as '+', the next distances are fifty metres, seventy metres (because it's easier to say than 75), 100, 150, 200, 300, etc.

Though there are standard variations on the corners, for example Long Fast Left, Fast Left over Crest – written as LFL and FL/C respectively – for every corner that you put in writing there are probably half a dozen variations which cannot be described. In your recce you must make efforts to memorize the roads. Even if you only drive over them once or twice, it is surprising how much sticks in your mind, particularly if you make frequent use of landmarks – for example 'Pole FL' if there is a telegraph pole just before a Fast Left.

Once you have established a system of notes to use (let us assume that it is my system), all that's left is hard work. At the beginning of the stage, stop the car. The co-driver should then write the name of the stage, its number and where he is starting the notes – for example, 'notes start at green gate on left'. Drive slowly and smoothly along the stage calling out the corners and the distances in the exact manner in which you wish your co-driver to write them down. Complete the stage and then return to the start and drive through it again, quite steadily, this time listening to the notes being read back to you by your partner in advance of the corners. Concentrate hard on what he is saying and as mistakes occur, which they will, give him the corrections. The more times you can drive over each stage the better. Every time you will change at least one corner or distance until the notes are nearly perfect – on the rally itself there will still be mistakes! Notes should always be made in daylight but where it is allowed to practise at rally speeds, the best, far safer time to practise them is at night.

Mastery of the pace note system is up to you. Application and practice will make almost perfect, but attention to relevant details and

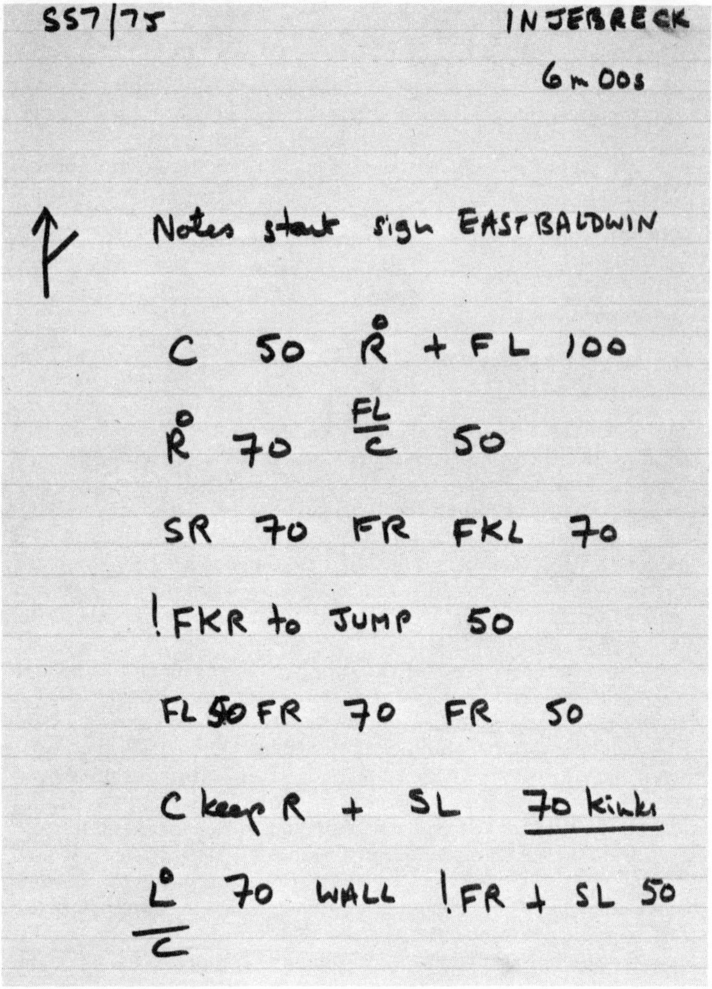

SS7/75   INJEBRECK

6 m 00 s

↑   Notes start sign EASTBALDWIN

C   50   R̊ + FL 100

R̊ 70 $\frac{FL}{C}$ 50

SR 70   FR   FKL 70

!FKR to JUMP   50

FL 50 FR 70   FR   50

C keep R + SL   <u>70 kinks</u>

$\frac{L̊}{C}$ 70   WALL   !FR ⊥ SL 50

A page of pace notes from the Manx Trophy Rally

accuracy are essential. Always record a corner faithfully even if there is no particular hazard: better to put a comment on the notes such as 'care bump'; and remember to make use of all the landmarks you can. One final point – there are very few drivers who drive to the letter of their notes, so if you can you will drive faster than they do.

Driving style with pace notes is somewhat different from driving blind because you know where you are going and what line you will be taking on a particular bend or brow. The car is set up in a more stable position, with very little need for the instability that is required for the unknown hazard. In fact you will be driving in an understeering condition more often than an oversteering one. This means, though,

Softly softly on snow (1971 RAC Rally)

that you are going relatively much more quickly and any deviation from your expected line could cause serious consequences simply because there is less of a safety margin.

Snow and ice rallies

The last type of rally to consider is the snow and ice event. A few years ago Swedish and Monte Carlo Rallies allowed free use of studded tyres but, because of environmental restrictions, the number and length of stud permitted has now been drastically reduced. Although tyre technology is advancing with great speed, ice is still a very slippery surface and although a multi-studded tyre provides excellent grip, the tyres that have to be used now call for much greater skill from the driver.

The secret on ice, with or without studs, is smoothness. No unnecessary sudden use of the steering, throttle or brakes. Remember that once you've locked up an unstudded tyre on ice by braking, it takes a second or two to start to revolve again when you have released the brake. Until it starts to revolve you will have no steering effect. Generally speaking, for this reason it is difficult to change direction in mid-corner, so the car should be set up in a smooth, power-on, tail-out position before the corner and balanced through it with the throttle only.

I did the Swedish Rally once and although I spent a lot of the time digging the car out of snowbanks (in a temperature of −30 degrees Centigrade), the experience of ice and snow was invaluable, and I thoroughly recommend a trip to Scandinavia to teach yourself the techniques involved. The only chance we have in the UK is once a year on the RAC Rally, which is just not enough.

Attitude

While on the subject of driving techniques, I should mention that perhaps the most important technique is in your head. Your mental approach to rallying in general, and in particular to attacking a special stage, can on its own make you drive quicker than your rivals. To succeed you must make yourself determined to be faster round the corner than the next man, to brake later than the next man, and, above all, to concentrate harder than the next man.

Taking part in rallies is a very expensive pastime, but in order to bring your driving up to a level where you can ask for a works drive without fear of embarrassment, you must take the risk of crashing, or at the very least leaving the road, in every event you enter. No amount of advice, or indeed practical instruction, can replace what you learn by merely driving quickly in competition with other drivers. How you react to the dashing of your hopes, especially if you dash them against a tree, is all part of the formative process.

6 *Rules and regulations, and rallies in general*
By MARTIN HOLMES

One of the curious things about rallying is that the only time you ever
learn about the rules is when you either organize an event or when you
have some trouble with the organizers and you wish to exercise what
you believe to be your rights. I suppose it can never be very easy to set
down the rules of a sport as complex as rallying in a very concise
manner, but nevertheless it is odd that magazines do not take time to
explain the more normal aspects of the rules so that beginners to the
sport can start off with a working knowledge.

British events

Motor sport in Britain is controlled by the Motor Sport Division of the
Royal Automobile Club in Belgrave Square, London. Rallies, racing,
autotests, trials, grasstrack, karts and sprints are all governed from this
division. General rules are published every two or three years in a
paperback publication called *Motor Sport Regulations* whilst detailed
alterations are listed annually in *Motor Sport Year Book*. The *Motor
Sport Regulations* places rules under various headings, such as 'General Competition Rules', 'Definitions', 'Event Organization and
Licences', and also under separate chapters where matters refer solely
to individual sports. These are standing rules that govern all rallies up
to national status. Only in specific and a strictly limited number of
cases can any of these rules be amended to suit the whims of individual
organizers. The rules govern not only how a rally (or other event)
should be run but also give instructions about cars, qualifications for
being granted licences, and a synopsis of the powers of government of
the RAC and the ways that the RAC can overrule organizers (or
competitors!) who step out of line.

Obviously there are many ways in which the rules of individual
events will vary, such as the time and place, the prizes, sometimes the
relative severity of individual penalties, the maps required, the names
of the officials, and so forth, and these are set out in the *Additional
Supplementary Regulations*. These vary for each event, and incorpo-
rate an entry form and indemnity clause which competitors have to
sign. They are usually published four to six weeks in advance, and
competitors are expected to apply for entry no later than seven to
fourteen days beforehand. The regulations are not particularly bulky,
since they only set out the rules particular to that event.

The delegation of the sport is carried out through individual clubs.

Clubs run events either singly or in conjunction with other clubs, and you must belong to a club that is specifically invited if you want to compete. This sounds like a closed shop and to a certain extent it is, but the range of clubs is pretty wide and they vary considerably in membership fees and attitudes. It is felt essential to have this sort of control to govern the sport properly, and an effective control is vital in gaining the approval of bodies such as the police. Obviously a local club is the first one you would wish to join and maybe like me you will be lucky enough to choose a club that will always suit your requirements; or you may soon meet people from other clubs which have more to offer you. You must belong to a motor club in order to compete in events right up to national level.

International events

The international scene is quite different, even for international events in your own country. Regulations, by comparison, come as fairly elaborate documents. Only the 'General Competition Rules' as set out in the *Motor Sport Regulations* will apply (and then only to British events – foreign events will have their own equivalent rules). All the

Common control boards of this sort are used on all FIA championship rallies

other rules for the event must be set out afresh. The general government of international rallies (and other motor sports) is ordered by the 'International Sporting Code' of the *Fédération Internationale de l'Automobile*, and although many attempts have been made to standardize regulations for international events, little so far has materialized beyond such features as common control warning boards. Control procedures are being standardized on continental rallies, but still they

54

are not universal and consequently they have to be set out and explained in detail every time. For home events your international licence is your passport for an entry, but for foreign events you also need a visa. This carries not only the approval of your governing body to the entry but also a certain degree of medical insurance.

The co-driver's role

Regulations, by virtue of their diversity, are the instruments of a co-driver's work. It takes experience to analyse regulations carefully, because so often material instructions appear through omission rather than by specific command. On the 1972 RAC Rally, road penalties were abandoned for the first time. The only way this was stated in the regulations was by omission of a penalty for being late at time controls! Only when you have read dozens of sets of regulations do you find it easy to spot variations like this – and then only if you take care.

When I am tired I find it is difficult to remember certain rules, even those which are obviously important because they are different from the normal ones. I find it is best to underline special rules in my personal copy of the regulations so that I know where to look to refresh my memory quickly. I also find on foreign events that certain rules are

---

G.—TIMING AND CONTROL OF THE RALLY

31. The average speed schedule on any highway not specially closed to the public will not exceed 30 m.p.h. A competitor found to have averaged more than 40 m.p.h. over a distance of not less than 20 miles on roads not closed to the public will be penalised. The actual arrival time at a Special Stage will not be used for the purpose of checking the average speed of a competitor from the previous Control or Stage.

Underline the rules you may wish to check again later

---

not known to marshals. In 1975 many rallies used a new rule stating that you could drive into a time control one minute before your due time of arrival, so that you could present your time card to the marshal at the exact moment that you were due. Many marshals, on several rallies, did not understand this, and the only way to persuade them that this practice was permitted was to compare the English edition word for word with the national edition of the regulations, and to underline the marshals' copy in the relevant place. The only trouble with this method is that the marshals then think you are proficient in their language and start a conversation!

Regulations are the basis of a competition. You must have complete command of them. Not only must you know what they say, you must also know very definitely what they do not say. And to be certain about the latter, you must be absolutely clear about amendments to the regulations. Some rallies are very haphazard about issuing amendments – and even cover themselves by stating that instructions can be published on official notice-boards and will be valid. Be very careful not to isolate yourself from other competitors, because you can be

1. Competitors should assemble in the collection area shown on page 10
    in the Road Book at least 30 minutes prior to their starting time on
    Saturday 22nd November. Starting time will in all cases be 09.00 hrs
    plus competitors number in minutes.

2. All competitors <u>must</u> sign the declaration on the reverse of their
    identification card and also write on that card the name and address
    of their Insurance Company.

3. Special Stage 6 - Olivers Mount, competitors will be required to drive
    one complete lap and an additional part lap of this stage. A drawing
    of the stage will be distributed at the start of the stage.

4. The route in the area of Special Stages 26 and 27 has been amended.
    Delete instructions from total mileage 38.86 on page 41 to total mileage
    50.23 on page 42 of the Road Book and replace with the following:

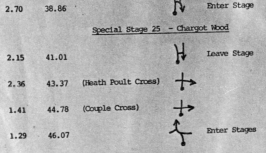

    2.70   38.86   Enter Stage

                    Special Stage 25 - Chargot Wood

    2.15   41.01   Leave Stage

    2.36   43.37   (Heath Poult Cross)

    1.41   44.78   (Couple Cross)

    1.29   46.07   Enter Stages

    N.B. The above distances are approximate.

    The entry and exit reference on page 5 of the Road Book should be replaced by

    SS 26   Entry at 181/970385
    SS 27   Exit at 181/873419

    The Time Schedule for the section from TC9 to TC10 remains unchanged.

5. Because of road re-construction, service can no longer be permitted on the
    road between Cerrigydrudion and SS43. A service area is now available after
    the Clocaenog Stages and this is on the left of the road immediately before
    the roundabout at total mileage 45.16 on page 58 of the Road Book.

certain that there will be some things of consequence that you have
missed simply because you were not in the right place at the right time.
Often casual conversation with an organizer will tell you of route
changes that will not be announced by bulletin until the next day. If
you did not hear of this change until later, you would probably not be
inconvenienced directly, but in the meantime you might well have
planned service crew schedules wrongly or made certain pace notes
unnecessarily. Always keep bulletins and amendments sheets together
so that any missing sheets will be immediately obvious. There are
many things which regulations do not tell you, but which you or your
entrant will need to know. The most usual query is what is the length
of asphalt stages and of loose-surfaced stages, and whether where one
type follows another there will be an opportunity to change tyres
between the two. This is crucial for the early planning of a rally. The
possibility of needing studded tyres is another point to raise. There is
always the possibility of freak weather conditions which catch out

foreigners, but what you can find out is how high the rally will be and whether snow is normal at that height at that time of year. Studs can often be used to good effect in conditions without snow or ice, but generally their use is best left to manufacturers' teams. For private teams it is an expense and an effort which is not worth while. In Britain the situation is clear. Studs are not allowed anyway.

Most foreign regulations set out the route and the timetable of the rally. This is most helpful as a prospective entrant can see immediately what sort of event it will be. The first point to establish is what the special stages will be like. Loose-surfaced or asphalt? Up-hill, up-and-down-hill, or mainly level? Straight or twisting? Will the emphasis be on power, strength of car or handling? Will the rally be a sprint or an endurance test?

Gradually the average European championship rally is being geared to minimal cost rallying, with cheap and easy training, ease of servicing, the opportunity to use the right tyres for the stages, and the use of just one base during the rally. Only the World rallies spare no efforts to make the rallies tough and expensive. Our RAC Rally must be the least expensive World rally to enter. In Finland, the Thousand Lakes competitors often cover 10,000 kilometres in training; entrants for the Monte Carlo Rally have to order hundreds of tyres studded in differing degrees; the Safari needs many service cars each covering thousands of kilometres, and so forth.

Most world championship rallies are killers on the cars and tyres

When you have a good idea about the stages take a close look at the road sections. In Britain the timing of road sections is something to take for granted; on the Continent it is vital to the structure of an event. You must consider carefully what sort of roads are used and what average speed is specified. How much time will be available for service? Is it worth taking spare gearboxes and axles, or will a delay of over ten minutes probably bring exclusion through lateness? Will there be a major service halt before the half-way halt? Will service cars be able to catch up with the rally route easily? On the Continent there is one major difference. Public roads are used for stages, so that service crews might have to travel considerably further from one point to the next than the competing car. Whereas a rally car might be sent along a road over a mountain, service cars will have to take an alternative route round the side.

You will need to investigate all these points before you leave to go on the rally, which means having a ready supply of the relevant maps at home. It never hurts to collect clean maps of areas used for rallies, simply so that you can plan future rallies at home – and it is difficult to obtain the right maps in another country. One advantage of rallying abroad is that you save considerably on the cost of maps; very few foreign maps cost anything like as much as British ones, and you need far fewer.

Once you have decided to enter a rally, be very clear with your driver about responsibility for correspondence, negotiations and paperwork generally. Rally organizers vary enormously in the degree in which they are prepared to help an entrant. Obviously you do not expect any assistance in entering an event in your own country, and clearly an organizer is more interested in negotiating terms of entry with a driver than with a co-driver. There are no rules about who does what, although most co-drivers are more methodical than drivers, and they are the ones who are ultimately expected to carry the responsibility for details; but drivers are normally the people who expect to set up deals. Any driver who expects to make his living out of rallying wants to keep his personal financial affairs to himself, and clearly this means that he will not want you to know everything; but short of this be certain that you know everything else that concerns the actual entry of the rally, including how many service cars there will be, whether they all will be carrying wheels, whether all the mechanics or friends are experienced, and what the travelling arrangements will be for the car – and for you.

Rallies for beginners

What sort of rallies can you enter? This depends on your licence and your driver's. To begin with you can only enter restricted or closed-to-club events. In theory this means local events, but in fact many of the leading events round the country are only of 'restricted' status. You will obviously gain the most satisfaction from events in which you have a sporting chance of success. Most clubs hold evening rallies of some two or three hours on public roads – events in which results are based on route-finding and unravelling the official instructions – but the minimum level of serious rallying is usually at restricted status. Both stage and road events can carry this status, and one of the best ways to find out about which events to enter is to hear about them through your club. Club magazines usually announce invitations, but often when it is too late for you to enter, so it is best to befriend your club's competition secretary so that you can have advance notice of possible forthcoming fixtures. The RAC *Motor Sport Year Book* includes a fixture list but this does not help much as it only specifies the name of the organizing club, the date and the status. Not only does it fail to say how important the event will be, or even whether it is a stage or a road event, but also this list is subject to considerable subsequent alteration. Clubs have trouble in obtaining authorization, or they cannot raise the necessary finance, or they fail to obtain the anticipated permission to use private land.

Championship events

After entering some smaller events, you will soon begin to get more ambitious. Small events are necessarily limited in their scope of territory and experience in organization. The stories in the magazines each week will entice you further afield. There is a considerable number of local and national championships which run events: the local events will be advertised in your club magazines and the national ones in the weeklies.

Whether you strive for a particular championship or simply find satisfaction in entering individual events knowing that championship status ensures a minimum standard or organization is up to you, but remember that the better the event the sooner people will enter, and unless you are a very important person your entry is likely to be taken on a 'first come first served' basis. Most championships need registration by competitors before you can count points, and often before you can enter at all, unless your own particular motor club is one of the clubs specially invited.

The major national championships include some really excellent events. There are two national road rally series, run by *Motoring News* and the BTRDA Club, but there are also several national stage rally championships. The monthly magazine *Cars and Car Conversions* holds a series for amateur drivers which struck fresh ground in rallying in 1975 by being decided on a class basis: Terry Kaby with a Mini Cooper won outright, because he was consistently best in his category. The next most important series is the 'Gold Star' championship run again by the BTRDA. One up from there is the Castrol/Autosport series, an interesting series which seeks to include events which use asphalt as well as loose-surfaced stage events; while at the very top is the national RAC series. These national series normally cost those who enter a lot of money, especially if big-engined cars that consume vast quantities of tyres are used – although Kaby's little Mini cost its owner a gross outlay of £700 for a whole season, and by the time prize

*Road rallies provide
inexpensive enjoyment*

*The BTRDA Gold Star
Championship often
provides spectacular
rallying (Malcolm Smith,
Ford Escort, Mexico)*

*The CCC series can be
very inexpensive – Terry
Kaby's Mini Cooper S*

money and sponsorship was taken into account it had cost a net total of
only £15. Depreciation of the car was not noted but a successful car
seldom depreciates in any case. Against these figures, the teams that
compete with Escorts on forest events often need budgets that extend
into five figures for a series of ten or fifteen home events.

Rallying abroad

Foreign rallying falls into three categories: non-championship, European championship and World championship. Generally the costs escalate accordingly. Because of the time involved it is unusual for any English team to set out to tackle a foreign series with a view of achieving success, although by virtue of a single foreign result and some good results in Britain the Irish driver Billy Coleman was fifth in the European championship in 1975. Normally you will try to compete on events which will give you the maximum amount of fun for a maximum opportunity of success (financial if possible) and a minimum outlay.

Some events assist a foreign competitor far better than others, and events with good sponsors are the best. European series events are many and various. They are held in many countries and carry a varying importance. The best and most established events carry a coefficient of four while the marginal events or ones that are new to the series have a coefficient of one. People contesting the series can score four times the points on the important events, three times on the next grade events and two times on the coefficient two rounds. These rallies are usually fairly short, two consecutive nights being a popular format. The World rallies tend to be longer, although one round, the *Tour de Corse* is only about twenty-five hours long. This is included in the series because it carries a high proportion of special stages and is incredibly tough. The Thousand Lakes is also just two nights long, but whereas most European events double up on the stages that are used, in Finland no stage is repeated so there is much more training to be done. (The RAC by comparison is two nights and five days.) In addition to these events there are certain publicity-orientated events. The British Tour of Britain started in this way before becoming a more serious event in its own right, while events like the Hong Kong and the Jamaica Rallies have often attracted a surprisingly high proportion of leading British entries, simply because of the local publicity that this brings the sponsors.

Tour of Britain Rally (John Cooper and Martin, BMW 3.0)

7 *Be prepared*
By CHRIS SCLATER

In this chapter I want to discuss the sort of final preparation which doesn't actually make the car any faster or more reliable but which can make a difference to your placing at the finish. Perhaps it may even enable you to reach the finish when without such preparation you would have to retire.

Driving position

Driving position is the most important factor for your own comfort. It will affect how tired you get after a few thousand miles of bumping and shaking around. Find a seat that fits you well. Although it must hold you tightly around the nether regions, it is more important to have good support for your thighs and some resistance to sideways movement of the upper part of your body. The thighs need good support to take the strain off the calf muscles. Because of the leverage exerted by your arms through your shoulders, if the upper part of the body is prevented from moving sideways the strain is taken off your stomach.

Once you have found a seat that suits you and is of a good strong construction, fit it into the car in a position to suit your legs. Forget about the steering wheel for the moment, and concentrate on fixing the seat at the best height for good visibility and then at the right distance from the pedals for your own comfort. Now, is the steering wheel at a comfortable distance? If you are tall, you will almost certainly say no, it's too far away – in which case you should find a wheel with a deeper dish or thicker boss. Most of the steering wheel makers have alternative wheels or bosses available. Avoid the straight-arm style of the racing driver – if you don't, the sort of leverage needed in rallying will soon wear out your shoulder muscles. Conversely, don't have the wheel too close – you will need room to swing your elbows around.

The gearlever is the next item. It may need bending close to you or perhaps lengthening. This is very much a personal choice, but it is always worth having the gearlever positioned in the right way for you.

The position of the throttle pedal can affect your ability to 'heel-and-toe' (the method of pressing the throttle pedal at the same time as braking). You will probably need to bend it nearer to the brake and perhaps lengthen it. Make sure there are no sharp edges on the pedals. During an event these will make your feet sore and in an accident could cause serious injury.

Pedals conveniently placed for heel and toe operation

Equipment in the car

Although the maplight is the province of the navigator, I am particular about its mounting point. Lights inside the car are very distracting and if you can reduce the reflections caused by the maplight so much the better. In every car I drive, the maplight is mounted on the door-shutting pillar above, and just behind, the co-driver's shoulder. Its natural position when clipped out of use should be forward along the roof or roll-cage, so that when it is pulled down for use it is fairly firm and doesn't shake about too much, as well as being as far away from the driver as possible. I try to fit a rheostat so that when the co-driver wants to read his pace notes on a special stage he can turn the light down so that it distracts me as little as possible.

A handle fitted to the roll-bar or the roof of the car can be useful for the co-driver to hold on to, but I find it distracting to see his arm out of the corner of my eye, and as modern seats and safety harnesses restrain movement, such a handle is a redundant item in the car anyway. If you

Maplight mounting

use an intercom to speak to each other without shouting (vital for pace notes) then the amplifier has to be mounted somewhere. The important thing is to keep the cables from your helmets to the amplifier well out of the way of arms and elbows and yet relatively easy to connect and disconnect. I always fit the amplifier to the back of the main hoop of the roll-cage with a jubilee clip. In this way the cable loops down from your helmet and up to the amplifier behind the line of the seats and causes no interference at all. Also, the cables are free of obstruction if you need to unplug and get out of the car quickly – in the case of a puncture, for instance.

While on the subject of helmets, I should add that there is nothing more annoying than a crash helmet rolling about in the back of a car on a road section. Apart from anything else, the microphone on your intercom can easily be damaged. Failure of the intercom could cause an accident. You must fit some sort of carrier for the helmets. There are various methods of doing this. I have even seen a plastic-waste-paper basket fitted to the floor of a works rally car just for this purpose. I prefer a foam-lined aluminium box of exactly the right size. A frame of small bore metal tubing, bent to fit inside your helmet and fixed to the back panel or roll-cage is just as good.

Whenever I see tools and jacks loose in the back of a rally car I cringe. I know of at least one rally driver who received a serious head injury when a loose metal object hit him during a bad accident. I remember preparing for the Manx in 1970 when my co-driver, John Davenport, went through the car with a fine-tooth comb, throwing out anything that was not firmly fixed down – from the first-aid kit to the smallest piece of dust. Always put tools in a tool roll and put them into a box or a soft bag which is attached securely to the floor of the car. If you can't put the jack in the boot then use over-centre clips or a leather strap to fix it. Do this, too, with the wheel-brace. Most works cars carry the wheel-brace inside the car, handy for the co-driver so that he can jump out and loosen nuts in the event of a puncture. But if the wheel-brace is not absolutely secure, it is one object that could hurt you badly should the car turn over.

Examine the inside of your car for any sharp projections, especially near your knees and feet. In my serious accident on the Scottish Rally in 1969, when the car was virtually destroyed, I was unhurt except for a cut knee caused by a mounting bracket for auxiliary switches mounted under the dash. This was all right when the car was upright, but when it turned over my leg dropped on to the sharp edge. Switches are best recessed into the fascia and within easy reach of the driver. Be sure that they are of several different shapes so that at night you know exactly which switch operates which component on the car. I always prefer to work the wipers and washers myself. By the time you've told your co-driver to work them you could have done it yourself. But – and this is very important – the operating switch must be very accessible and easy to find. Apart from the dip-switch, horn and indicators, it's the only switch you might have to use when on the move. For this reason it

should be as easy to find as the gearlever.

Different shapes for switches – easily accessible

Personal Protection

Of prime importance in the preparation of car and driver is personal protection. A full roll-cage goes without saying and we have discussed the dangers of sharp projections in the car. Wear flame-proof overalls and gloves. The gloves are very comfortable and last a long time. They are also useful if there is an engine problem which may involve work near a hot exhaust. Frank Gardner even won a saloon car race at Brands Hatch because of Nomex gloves. The hot exhaust had started a fire when oil leaked into the car and he kept it under control by beating it with his glove between gear changes!

Obviously your crash helmet must comply with latest regulations. If you have an intercom with a boom microphone, then the boom should be angled toward the inside of the car. For a driver of a right-hand drive car, it should be on the left-hand side of your helmet. In this way the cable doesn't have to cross over behind your back to the amplifier and, more important, there is no danger of the boom catching on the roll-cage. I use an open-face helmet in preference to the integral type for greater comfort on long rallies, particularly in high temperatures. A lot of drivers prefer the integral type, but it is certainly a very individual choice.

Shoes and socks are also a personal choice, but remember that you must wear shoes that will remain comfortable for up to two or three thousand hard miles. Never wear nylon socks because they will melt in the event of fire and cause nasty injuries. Rather wear Nomex socks or any bleached wool type. Some of the dyes used in coloured ones can infect the blood if you are cut through the sock.

A final safety feature – and certainly the most important – is your safety harness. There are some harnesses available which tend to come **65** loose. These should be avoided at all cost. Without doubt the best, and most expensive, type available is the Willans. It is constructed on the principle of the parachute harness, very easy to get out of and very comfortable. It is naturally a full harness type, with each shoulder strap pushing into the main buckle individually. The lap strap – which can be used on its own if required – should be fitted to restrain your thighs in a vertical plane, rather than your stomach in a horizontal one. Serious injury to your relatively soft stomach can be caused by a badly fitted belt. The shoulder straps which normally combine into one behind the seat should pass back from your shoulders at an angle of forty-five degrees. In this way, vertical movement is restrained without the risk of compression of your spine should you have a severe head-on accident. So many people mount the shoulder strap eye on the floor directly behind the seat. In a frontal accident your body tends to move forward and the inevitable result is to force your shoulders down.

A boom-fitting microphone on Chris's crash helmet

Correct fitting for the Willans harness

Punctures and wheel changes

I have mentioned the jack and the wheel-brace, and it would be as well to discuss how to use them in a hurry. Despite significant advances in tyre design, punctures still occur. Admittedly, the most common cause for a puncture is driver error – hitting a rock or a log, for instance. When the tyre actually goes flat you must have a pre-arranged plan to deal with the situation.

Even after practice, it will take at least two minutes to change a wheel and be back on the move again. You must decide whether or not, if you continue to the end of the special stage, the puncture will reduce your speed sufficiently for you to lose more than two minutes. If it will, then stop and change. If in doubt, continue, because two minutes is a very good time in ideal conditions (though it is unlikely that you will have ideal conditions on a rough special stage). The one saving factor is the use of spectators to help lift the car and to help you by holding lamps in the dark. So if you have to stop, try to do so near spectators. All you then have to do is change the wheel – the jack can stay where it is in the car.

Once the decision to change has been made, the pre-arranged plan must be carried out smoothly and without panic. First the co-driver unhooks the intercom leads before the car has stopped. He then gets out with the wheel-brace and loosens the wheel nuts. The driver, meanwhile, fetches the jack and starts to raise the car. While he's doing this the co-driver gets the spare wheel and changes it over. If it's dark, one of you must have a torch. Lower the jack, check the nuts and you're on your way again – but don't forget to do up your safety belts.

It's certainly worth practising wheel changes in the garage before the rally. Your co-driver may not be familiar with the car and those two minutes could easily stretch to five. Before every rally you must check that the jack is working properly. On one Sherry Rally that I did in Spain, the leading works SEAT car had a puncture and his jack wasn't working – it cost him a win.

The throttle

Constant attention to the throttle-operating mechanism is vital, whether it be a mechanical linkage or a cable. Be sure that you are getting full throttle and that the pedal is touching a stop when you have that full throttle opening. If you don't have a stop, the chances are the mechanism will be under strain and if you're using a cable there is likelihood of a breakage. To be sure that no time is lost in that event, it is advisable to have a double cable fitted – the second cable just a bit slacker than the first. The only time I had a cable break was on the Total Rally in South Africa. It was a twenty-five kilometre stage and it happened after about five. Six minutes to fit a new cable cost us at least two places. With a double cable I would have had no problem.

Brakes

The most frightening accident in my life happened because of a lack of thoroughness on my part. It was on the TAP Rally in Portugal in 1971 when I was driving an Escort with Henry Liddon. The first special stage was very fast with only about half a dozen brake applications – but they were very hard applications. The finish was at the end of a half-mile straight and the road went sharp right soon after. Straight ahead was a steep bank about fifteen feet high with a wall at the bottom. We flew along the straight at about a hundred miles an hour, over the finishing line, hit the brakes – nothing! I suppose the car slowed to about seventy to eighty miles an hour, but we were heading for the wall with no chance of stopping or turning right. I remember screaming, because I was sure it was the end. The next thing was the dust settling and we were perched on top of the bank without a scratch. The car was a few inches shorter, however. The wall was of the dry stone variety and had given way fairly easily. The bank had absorbed our speed quite smoothly and slowed the car down to about ten miles an hour as we cleared the top.

68   All this happened because I had not 'faded' the new brake pads

properly. When you fit new competition brake pads you could have the same frightening experience if you don't fade them deliberately. My method for fading is to go out on a straight open road which is fairly free of other traffic. Drive along in second or third gear at nearly maximum revs and use the left foot to work the brake pedal. Press it really hard until you start losing the pedal and the brakes fade. There will also be a 'hot brakes' smell. Let them cool down and then do it again. You should then have good brakes however much punishment you give them.

The balance of the braking ratio is important. With this it is possible to change the bias from the front to the back very simply. It is possible to vary the ratio on a standard car by changing the size of the rear wheel cylinders – the larger the wheel cylinder the more braking effort.

A production car is generally built with a bias on the front brakes. This is the safest set-up, but for the proficient rally driver not necessarily the quickest. On loose surfaces the brakes can be used, if balanced correctly, to set the car up for a corner. By adjusting the system to cause the back wheels to lock just before the front, the unbalanced condition can be induced without the need for the 'swing'. In addition, if you are caught out by a tightening corner, a dab on the brakes will bring the back of the car out a bit further, thus inducing the oversteer condition.

I would stress that this is a technique which must be treated with caution. Application of brakes set up in this way when you are travelling at high speed on an icy straight could cause a disastrous spin. It is a technique which should be practised where you have plenty of room to spare!

The ideal way of adjusting the ratio is with a valve to reduce the pressure in one of the brake lines (either back or front). The amount of variation they give is small, however, so you should have the ratio very near to the desired balance before you fit the valve. The other method as used on the works Escorts is with a balance bar system. A separate master cylinder is used for front and rear brakes and they are operated by a bar which pivots on a rose joint fixed to the brake pedal. By winding the bar across, the mechanical leverage on each cylinder is altered. Brake balance is an important contribution to a well-built car.

Weight and balance

Some of the most successful cars in rallying have had engines over the driven wheels: the Mini, Imp, Porsches, Alpines, and more recently the Lancia Stratos. Handling and road holding are important but clearly the big advantage of this configuration is the ability to transmit the power on to the road surface. The weight is in the right place.

The inherent balance of a car is also important. The best balanced car of the front-engined, rear drive configuration that I have driven is the Toyota Corolla. On the other hand some drivers feel that the Datsun 240Z is front-heavy. The Ford Escort is also a well proportioned car. In competition over the years the weight was reduced on the front or moved to the back, and where possible removed completely. **69**

For instance, the battery and dry sump oil tank are mounted in the boot. The car now has an aluminium cylinder block and the resulting saving in weight allows for a lighter, thinner sump-shield to be fitted.

Weight-saving has two advantages – the car is lighter and therefore faster, and, just as important, there is less stress on the mechanical parts of the car – transmission, suspension and so on. The first Datsun Violet was a classic example of overweight. The car had been built to withstand the sort of treatment that a tank-testing ground might give it. Steel brackets had been used where aluminium ones would have been adequate. The carrier for the spare wheel weighed nearly as much as the spare itself, and the sumpshield was twice as thick as was necessary. The Japanese engineers had built the car with the Safari in mind. But, of course, European events are sprints compared to the Safari, which is more of an endurance event. Look at your own car. There will always be ways of saving weight and even small savings add up to a considerable amount.

Lights

Lights are very much a personal choice. I find that foglights are as useless in fog as any other light. The important thing about lights in fog is that they should be pointing down so that the fog doesn't throw back reflections. You need as much light as possible on a clear night and to have lights pointing down in case of fog is a waste of valuable wattage. It is better to use dipped headlights only in fog, and four spotlights in addition to headlights for clear conditions. I always set my lights on a beam-setter straight ahead. Headlights give a good general light and the spotlights give the range that you need for high-speed driving. If the fog looks like being solid all night, then adjust your lower spotlights so that they point down at the road about twenty yards from the car. It doesn't take two minutes to do and the spotlights can easily be reset when the fog clears. When you set your lights before the rally remember to do it with full equipment on board, half a tank of petrol and preferably two people as well.

Tyres

Tyres have proved to be a very decisive factor in rally results and tyre development is a rapidly advancing science. A tyre of racing construction was first used on a major loose-surface rally by Ford on the 1975 RAC. It proved to be very successful under certain conditions, and was probably the greatest advance in tyre design for use in competition for many years.

Racing tyres are very expensive, and a racing tyre adapted for the forest is beyond the reach of the private entrant's pocket. However, rallies are won and lost on the choice of tyres, and comparing the cost of tyres to the cost of the engine puts their importance in perspective. You must realize that tyres are as vital as the horsepower your engine produces and could probably cost as much as your engine in one year.

Racing tyres are essential for competitive tarmac driving

When you enter an event, try to find out the surfaces that will be used. How many of the stages are tarmac, and how many are loose? Using a forest tyre on tarmac can cost you up to fifteen to twenty seconds a mile against those who have racing tyres. You don't have to be Einstein to work out that even a modest amount of tarmac on a predominately loose rally could cost a place or two at the final reckoning.

The more powerful your car, the more the racing tyre pays off on tarmac. The rate of wear is significantly less per mile than the knobbly tyre in the forest. In fact, when I did the Manx Rally in the Datsun Violet, six Goodyear racing tyres covered the whole event. I would have needed at least ten radials for the same distance and with the racing tyres costing about fifty per cent more, the bill for both types would have been very similar. So, when you prepare your car and team for a season of rallying, don't penny-pinch on tyres for the sake of a few extra horsepower. Tyres are now a deciding factor in results and it's worth having the right equipment for the job you're doing.

I remember the Firestone Rally in 1975. It was held at the end of March in northern Spain. I had driven the rally twice before and had

Meeting unexpected snow on the 1975 Firestone Rally

been successful. This time the entry was better – works Alfas and Fiat-Abarths as well as Billy Coleman's Escort and a number of top French and Spanish crews. My preparations were good, I thought. Racing tyres and knobblies, two good mechanics, a fully equipped service car and a recce car from England. A professional entry. But I was caught out in the biggest possible way. The night before the rally started there was heavy snow on the higher sections and then a sharp frost – and we had no studded tyres. The works cars all had studs available and for the locals it was straightforward to arrange for tyres to be collected. We were a thousand miles from home and totally unprepared for the expense of buying Firestone studded tyres at £40 per tyre. The silly thing was that I could easily have brought some with me from England, but the thought of snow in Spain hadn't entered my mind.

As it turned out luck was with us. There were some notable retirements among the top crews and we finished third – better than I could have hoped for without the snow. But it so easily could have been tenth, and I could have lost a lot of prize money. I had learnt a lesson – and I hope it illustrates the point.

8 *Frightened?*
By MARTIN HOLMES

'Don't you ever get frightened?' is the usual question. 'Not at all,' I reply, 'You need brains to appreciate the dangers involved.' Yes, it is possible to hurt yourself in any car, but the development of rally cars over the past few years has lessened this possibility to a remarkable degree.

It is never a good idea to brag about your immunity from harm and it is exceptionally silly not to take personal safety precautions. By and large, however, if you take all the reasonable precautions you can, you will be unlikely to come to harm. Cars have hoops inside the body to help retain the shape of the passenger compartment. This has two advantages. First, the compartment does not compress and therefore trap you inside, and second, the doors do not distort and fly open. Safety belts are of the full harness type which stop your body from slipping out of place if the impact comes at an unusual angle, such as on the roof instead of head-on. Crash helmets are required to comply with specifications that are improved at frequent intervals. On serious events we almost always wear fire-proof overalls, the only exception being events in very high temperatures where there is an overriding safety hazard of being too hot inside a car. Laminated windscreens are compulsory.

What happens in a crash? First of all, I shut my eyes! Very seldom does a co-driver know more than a second in advance that there is going to be an accident. The more skilled the driver, the more the driver can fight for control of his car long after a less experienced driver has given everything up for lost. It's almost like the bullet that kills you: you never hear it coming! This in many ways is a very good thing, because you should not be in any more state of tension than normal. (You probably know that rugby football players are tackled by surprise, when they are relatively relaxed, whereas soccer players are tackled in moments of tension. As a result there are far more injuries incurred by the soccer players than by the rugby players.)

The things that can cause you unnecessary injury are objects flying around in the car. Most big rallies issue competitors with small zip-bags, and these are excellent for carrying small items which might otherwise come loose. Sharp objects in front of you can cause cuts and bruises, especially to the legs, while I shudder to think of the damage that the sharp end of a pencil could cause. Loose belts are a hazard, particularly if you hit an object head-on very hard, while things which I

Left: The foam padding around the rectangular fuel injector selector box was not sufficient to stop a bad bang on the legs. The tape over the switches was not a safety measure – it was to stop crews trying to 'tune' the engine in mid-rally!

Right: The danger of intercom leads which do not readily unplug is shown in this Thousand Lakes Rally picture. Jussi Kynsilehto is helped out of the car

am always worried about are intercom leads which do not unplug easily, and the string retaining stopwatches which many co-drivers carry around their necks.

I know quite a number of rally co-drivers who have lost their nerve in accidents, and on every occasion when I have tried to find out why their final rally accident was any worse than the others they have been unable to say. I think that many people hurt themselves because they hold themselves in awkward positions. I have seen co-drivers spread-eagle their arms inside a rally car in such a way that injury is inevitable if there is an accident. It is always possible to lower a seat, even in Group 1, so you are sitting nearer the floor. This immediately gives the impression of a bigger passenger compartment for a co-driver, which must be safe in an accident, quite apart from giving your driver more room to move. Not only this, but also it is usually necessary to move a seat back so your leg-straps fit better and do not ride up your clothing.

I hurt my neck on the first big jump that I had on the Thousand Lakes Rally. It was thoughtlessness: it was simply a matter of my

looking down at the moment of impact with the ground, instead of ensuring that the shock from my head was taken down the spine to the seat. I was winded when a Mini in which we had lost our brakes on the long fast main road through the centre of Dalby Forest crashed at the T-junction at the end – and this was because the belts we were using were of the type that gradually slip and are never properly tight when

Good seats and good belts make it now unnecessary for co-drivers to hold on tight – unless the seat itself breaks

No need to hold on tight – if your belts are right.

they are actually needed. You can only relax in a car when the belts are really tight. It is interesting that few co-drivers nowadays hold on to their grab-handles any more. This is a sure sign that belts and seats have improved over the years.

Accidents are never funny, but when the financial shock has worn off they can often prove the source of amusing if not actually instructive comment. I once navigated for Denis Cardell who is now well respected and indeed a member of the RAC Rallies Committee, but who had a reputation for his accidents. He wore glasses, and had a novel method of telling how serious his accidents were without having to get out and examine his car. A slight accident, and his glasses remained on his head. A bad one which would require immediate repair to the car would cause his glasses to leave his head and fall on the floor of the car, and a terminal accident would be signified by the destruction of his glasses!

The Thousand Lakes Rally in 1975 ended for Jussi Kynsilehto and me on stage 23 with an accident which strangely enough was even less painful (for me) than the jump we had experienced on stage 2. Even as we flew through the air for our final time I had no idea that things were other than normal: it was only an unusual crashing motion that caused me to stop reading the pace notes and look up at the road. We came to an eventual stop and I was puzzled that spectators bothered to open the door and try to pull us out of the car. As crashes went, it had not seemed all that severe. Why weren't they pushing us back on to our wheels so we could drive on our way? Eventually I saw the reason all too clearly. There were hardly any wheels left on the car, and those that were pointed in some curious directions. It is impossible to tell just how serious an accident has been until you study the car. That head-on in Dalby in the Mini should have been a final, mortal blow, but in fact the car started immediately, and we continued for another twelve hours. We eventually retired through falling too far behind time. We had to go slowly for so long because we could not find the hole in the brake pipe.

Accidents are always very upsetting, even to co-drivers who do not have the troubles of taking the wreckage back home and the cost and labour of repair. Sometimes accidents are almost inevitable. Chris will probably excuse my relating the story of the 1969 Scottish, which he tackled in his old Mark 1 Lotus Cortina and in which he was incredibly successful, even when ranged against the new Escort TCs. Earlier in the year, Chris and I had finished second on the Welsh, beaten only by Ove Andersson with a Group 5 works Escort TC although for the Scottish he had taken another co-driver (Peter Valentine). Before the rally my last word of goodwill to Chris was to let me know when the inevitable accident occurred. Three days later, his very first words over the telephone were: 'It happened last night'. He had been doing even better than on the Welsh – he had been actually leading the Scottish before the car left the track, flew over the edge of the track for fifty feet before landing on its roof in the trees.

Accidents are inevitable in the career of any driver who seeks to be better than his rivals. Only by driving over your limit can you discover where your personal limits lie. On the other hand, only drivers who learn from their accidents and do not constantly drive over their limit are good and useful.

Strangely enough, it was only because of someone else's accident that Chris and I came to be involved in each other's rallying. Peter McDowell and I had been in quite a major incident with a Mark 1 Lotus Cortina on the Isle of Wight in 1967 when we uprooted a substantial gate-post and severely damaged the car in the process. To me the major disappointment was that the rally had been a *Motoring News* championship round (in those days they included stage events), which we had been leading comfortably, and that I had never won one of those events before. The car which before the accident had been a pretty good specimen now needed rebodying, and the only available bodies in those days were second-hand ones. After the work had been done, Peter lent Chris the car for the Gulf-London. I am sure that would never have happened if it had been still a smart car.

In general, pace note rallies are faster, but usually safer, rallies than secret route ones. More accidents occur on pace note events through bad note-making than for any other reason, and therefore your safety is very much in your own hands. The Eppynt ranges in the Brecon area of Wales have seen some remarkable shunts, but nearly always they have occurred at places where the wise and knowledgeable would have eased their feet off the accelerator. Sudden ice is one of the really bad experiences for a rally driver, and this is why competitors on the Monte Carlo Rally take great pains to ensure someone checks their pace notes before a stage is run, to mark where this ice is lying. Both the Renault-Alpine and the Lancia teams lost two cars through crashes at the same bend on the 1975 Monte Carlo Rally because ice had spread further than when the notes were checked.

Pressure and tiredness are the other main causes of accidents on pace note events. Reading notes is an art which needs experience and a clear mind: a driver can easily tell when a co-driver is getting drowsy, as can a co-driver tell when a driver is getting tired. When both partners work well there is a rhythm which leads to incredible smoothness in driving, and very fast times, but the moment one bend is badly read or badly noted that rhythm is broken, and it takes a long time to restore. Tiredness can lead to sudden breakdown in concentration and a late instruction, or even a completely wrong instruction. If a driver senses a co-driver has lost his edge he should say so without delay: usually the shock of being told to wake up by a driver is quite sufficient warning. Pressure is something you either revel in or you cannot stand. It strikes people in different ways. On secret rallies pressure does not have a very drastic effect. Usually it results in some untidy lines round corners which lead to bad times and little worse. But with pace note rallies, an untidy line will usually lead you straight off the road.

What should a co-driver do when you have an accident? First, consider your situation. Immediately, so far as possible, ascertain the damage to the car. Second, consider exactly where you are, and how near you are to help. Even when you are in the middle of some huge forest complex on a secret route rally, you should try to follow your position on a map in case you need to start looking for help. Many forest routes loop around in circles, so that when you are half-way through a long stage you may be very near to civilization. Next you must decide what to do. If a car cannot be extricated under its own power and with your assistance after four or five attempts, further attempts will probably make eventual extrication more difficult.

Remember that people who go out specially to watch a rally are far more willing to muck in and help you get going again than luckless country folk who never asked for your rally to come past in the first place. Chris and I crashed on the last morning of the 1971 Circuit of Ireland. It was not a bad accident, and there was no damage at all; it was simply that the car was in a swamp and needed dragging out. We needed help from the spectators. Money seemed to be the answer. I reached into my pocket and waved a £10 note in the air. If our car was back on the road within five minutes, that £10 note was to be theirs. Not a movement. Not a flicker of an eyelid. Eventually it was only by some physical persuasion that our desperation was made plain and action resulted. We later asked Ronnie McCartney if this was normal in Eire. 'Well yes,' he explained, 'they never asked the rally to come past, and to them your little escapade was probably all part of the act. They did not know what was really happening.' Very plausible. Only later did I realize what was probably the real reason for their hesitation in helping. It had been an English £10 note.

Don't stand there doing nothing!

There are many 'don'ts' about post-accident car recovery. Don't plaintively wave a rope in the air, hoping that another competitor will stop and help you, unless you are really, absolutely desperate. You wouldn't stop for them, unless you had decided to retire, would you? We have done this ourselves (Dovey, Datsun 240Z, RAC 1974) and heard all the ribald comments in the bar afterwards. We've seen other people in a similar position (Fowkes, Ystwyth, Welsh 1970) and been hard pressed to contain our mirth. Don't laugh too loud when you see some rival in trouble. Jussi Kynsilehto burst out laughing when we saw Blazej Krupa's Renault in a heap beside the road on the 1975 Warsaw Rally – and within five seconds our axle had seized! Don't stand there doing nothing. If there is nothing else that you and your driver can think of doing, then one of you must go off and find some help. Never both go off, and never go for long. If in doubt whether to go back or forward, always go forward, just in case your driver gets going without your help and can then drive down the track to find you. The main difficulty over getting spectators to help is instilling in them your personal sense of urgency. With the adrenalin working overtime, you can run two miles in search of help, but they won't willingly run two miles back to help you unless they can really understand your predicament.

Another don't: don't ever turn your back on oncoming cars – even if spectators are waving them down

It is difficult to grip a rally car

Always attach a rope to one of the towing eyes on your car when you leave the road and are waiting for help. Ten people can pull on a rope. Perhaps the biggest trouble in de-ditching a rally car is for people to get a firm grip on it, either to push it horizontally or to lift it. I have often wondered why cars don't have more devices to enable them to be man-handled – but then that would defeat the object of the exercise. There is always a big to-do when sufficient help does come to hand. Everybody wants to do things different ways. It is a common sight to look up and see people pulling a car in opposite directions. Being essentially an idle person, I like to assume command of such a situation and give the orders, become a sort of cheer-leader if you like. It means that there is one person fewer to do the pulling or pushing, but at least it means that the efforts of the others will be harnessed more usefully.

If and when you get going on the rally after a major incident, it is very difficult to settle down to a routine again. Always there is something amiss with the car, even if it is just the steering, and always there is complete disorder inside the car. Your driver's shoes will be muddy, the lights will probably be broken or badly adjusted and you will usually have a major psychological battle to fight with depression. If you find clutching at straws any use, remember it is always possible that the stage might be cancelled. If you prefer to face the reality of defeat, remember that now you will have little to lose, so maybe it is time to try for a few fastest times. And if facing reality means recogniz-

ing that retirement is inevitable, be sure that you make the most of a

If your own retirement is inevitable, maybe there is some other poor fellow to help . . . Hannu Mikkola on this occasion

bad job, that you hand in your time cards for the stages which you completed, and that you explain your predicament to the members of the motoring press at the finish. Remember also to collect your belonging from the car – it may be the last time you see it.

Accidents occur often but seldom lead to injury. The quotations for personal accident insurance are proof enough of that. Always remember that they can occur and will undoubtedly occur at the least convenient moment. Pilots of single-engined aeroplanes often cast their eyes over likely looking fields as they fly, just in case they need to use one for an emergency landing. Being prepared for a bang and wondering what you would do if one occurred is just one of the things a co-driver should have at the back of his mind. Be prepared, and it will surely never happen!

There's nothing worth taking from that wreck! (Brecon Forest, 1967)

9 *From theory to practice*
By MARTIN HOLMES

Advance planning

Most rallies begin as ideas in the back of the mind. Often they are the result of coincidence: two things happen and suddenly a latent thought becomes an obsession. Sometimes you are involved in a championship so you know in advance which events you want to do, other times events are one-offs. Whichever it is, it is most important to work out an annual calendar of events before a season even begins. Seasons run from January through to December, more as a matter of convenience than anything else, since there is no closed season these days. A wall-planner chart is excellent for a rally calendar. At a glance you can see how close individual events will be. It is a good idea to mark events in various championships in different colours so you can see easily if one event is included in more than one series, and also if one championship often has events which clash with bigger rallies, and which consequently may be poorly supported. Plotting events on a big chart will also show up those one-off events which can easily be fitted in within a different series.

Choosing an event

There is always a definite moment when you become determined that you will enter one particular event, sometimes early in the year, sometimes very late. Availability of a car and availability of funds are the usual hurdles to overcome. Suitability of a car is often a subject less often considered, and there are many missed opportunities because of this. All the internationals and nowadays most of the one-day events as well have a comprehensive class system. If you are a racing enthusiast, you will know that you can easily have eight or ten winners in a day's sport, but in rallying the overall winner is the only winner. Classes in rallies balance this inequality. Gradually the expense of aiming at outright winning, together with the unlikelihood of a newcomer succeeding in any case, has made classes more popular. One way to discover good classes is to look through rally results and see the class winners. Look for the classes where the winners score colossal points compared with the usual number of penalties: a sure sign that there are few good drivers in that class. Even with slow cars, a good driver will score penalties reasonably near the top ten positions. If you have the

An excellent 'class car' is the Clan Crusader – when there is a separate category for cars up to 1000 c.c. It is equally at home on road or stage events. (Alan Conley and Martin on the 1973 Illuminations Rally)

chance, study entry lists of past events as well, and see how many enter these classes, and what cars they drive. Always aim to gain some lasting achievement from a rally. If you cannot sensibly aspire to a top position, a class position is a good ambition.

Finance

Availability of money is quite a different subject. Chris discusses budgeting generally in Chapter 10. Obviously it is unlikely that you will know where every penny will come from before you decide to enter a rally: indeed few sponsors are interested in people who do not possess the burning determination to compete. Just cast a glance at the regulations, in due course, to see what are the conditions for withdrawing an entry if need be. Often you will be thinking about an event long before the regulations appear. You will need to save up, you will certainly need to book holidays or time off for a major event. Most of the expenses will be pretty clearly identifiable from a previous year's event, subject to the usual increases for inflation. If possible, talk to people who have entered the event before to discover whether your assumptions are correct. Can you manage with just one service crew? Is it false economy to use cheap hotels outside town, for instance?

Regulations

When the regulations appear, you can really get to work. These are a few things you will immediately look to see:

Dates: Have they changed from the original calendar?

Status: Will you have the correct licences? If not, will you or your partner have time to obtain the right grade before the event?

Classes: Will you have a good chance in your class? Are there any horrible clauses saying that classes might be merged if insufficient people enter? If so is the word 'may' used? A good idea is to contact the organizers to find out if 'may' will be implemented. You are often given the right to withdraw but by that time you will be completely committed to competing in other respects. Furthermore, are the prizes for classes and lower-placed finishers well distributed, or will just the top few crews take all the money?

Entry fees: Were your original estimates correct? Do they jump nastily after a certain date?

Surfaces: How many different types of tyres will have to be bought?

Choice of entries: Is it first-come, first served, or will organizers select who starts if there is over-subscription? In other words, is there a rush to put your money down?

Range of maps required: Are there many maps, indicating that the service cars may have more travelling than usual? Check that the start and finish are in the same place, and that there is not a night or long halt in some other town.

Timetable: Check timetable of rally, to see what time off work is required.

Insurance: Can the organizers help, and if so how much notice do they want? Many foreign organizers deal with this automatically, but not all.

Armed with this information you have the essential items which will tell you if the rally is a viable proposition for you or not. Obviously there may be special rules that need careful interpretation, which may also alter the decision on entering, or the choice of type of car. These are mainly foreign event factors: things like limits on studs or practising may easily change your plans appreciably. While these various points are dealt with, your driver will also be rounding up support for service crews and you as co-driver will be reading the regulations further.

The weeks before the start are the time to think about the regulations, not the moments just before the 'off'. Where are the time controls? Are they at the start of every stage or simply at isolated places? How late can you be at stages – if you are late at one stage, can you make good the lateness and arrive at the next on time? (British rallies are very woolly about these rules.) What rallying will there be in darkness? Do you have to bring your competition numbers? Are there particular places on the car where stickers must not be placed? Are cars locked away in a *parc fermé* (sealed car park) after scrutineering – and if so for how long?

See how the route uses identical roads on occasions. On the event in question, this was far from obvious in the regulations.

If the rally route is given in the regulations, you have a lot more additional work to do. Some rallies prepare coloured maps showing different stretches of the route on different pages, forgetting to mention that the maps are of the same, or substantially the same, area, so that in fact the route twists round itself in one huge knot. Before you go to practise the route, you will have to transpose all these maps on to one master plan so you do not miss the chance to make notes when you drive along. If you have been lucky enough to go to the Isle of Man for the Manx Trophy Rally, you will probably recall just how confusing are the road closure orders, how difficult it is to plan a journey for a service car – or even for a spectators' car – without running foul of closed roads. The Manx Rally uses roughly four laps of the island. Some rallies are even more confusing. The Elba Rally uses about eight laps of the island, for instance. I mentioned in Chapter 6 the various other things you will have to think about, particularly if the route is in the regulations as well.

Scrutineering before the 1975 Sherry Rally

Scrutineering

Scrutineering sometimes takes place immediately before the start, sometimes earlier. Sometimes the competing crew have to attend, in order to sign the various indemnity forms, whereas at other times it is quite permissible for mechanics or friends to deal with this chore, thus giving the crew a chance to enjoy a few more hours' sleep before the event.

Regulations usually put great importance on the time for reporting for scrutineering, and it is usually wise to ask organizers beforehand if this is a rigid timetable, particularly if you cannot work on the car between scrutineering and the start. If you have some last-minute work to carry out on the car and there is a *parc fermé*, it is sometimes best to arrive at scrutineering with some essential detail on the car defective, and be failed. You will then be invited to return when the detail is rectified. Make sure, of course, how long the scrutineers will wait for you.

Try to deal with all the documentation at the offices of the organizers if they have headquarters which are open before scrutineering takes place. This will save you from the otherwise inevitable panic with hundreds of pieces of paper, official stickers, gratuitous stickers, amendments, further amendments and all the other confusions of the moment. The odds are against your arriving first time with all the paperwork that is wanted, anyway.

In the hectic few days before the start, make certain you keep track of time. Do not emulate my driver on the Portuguese Rally who eventually took me aside and asked why our mechanics were working so furiously on his rally car. His face was a picture when I explained the start was merely three hours away. After all the rush of training, he had in his mind that the start was the following day!

Furthermore, do not rely on mechanics to adhere to any strict timetable. There is no point in holding a post-mortem after an event in which, because someone else could not produce your car on time, you were forbidden to start on time. Mechanics, and team managers, can easily get distracted by an emergency. Many rallies have exclusion penalties for lateness at the start, others reserve the right to exclude if this allows a reserve to start instead.

Pre-rally rest

The ease with which we sleep before the start of a rally depends largely on our pattern of living in the days beforehand. Many professional drivers make sure that they carry out their practice at night in the week before the start, not simply because by then they have made their notes and now they wish to perfect them by driving at competition speeds; it also helps their bodies to adjust to a routine of night driving and day-time sleeping. For day events sleep is no trouble, except that you may well have a long drive to the start the night before and feel loath to rise early. Be certain you do not give in to the temptation to be too sociable the night before, even if certain leading drivers reckon they drive faster with a hangover. They are leading drivers because they can drive fast despite a hangover!

Always carry an alarm clock you trust – even the most switched-on hotels or kindliest landladies get overwhelmed by breakfasts at 5.30 a.m. If you have a rally where you can sleep in a hotel at a rest halt, take the precaution of getting your colleagues to wake each other – and to knock until the person actually gets up. Nothing is more deadly than being woken after a couple of hours sound sleep – but ultimately few things are more rewarding in terms of maintaining strength. Sleep in cars or on hotel chairs or floors is no substitute.

The service crew

One of the worst ways to start a rally is for your service crew to forget to leave ahead of you. This is most easily done at early morning starts. Remember that although they will probably be able to cover ordinary road sections at the same speed as rally cars, you in the rally car may wish to make up time. It may also be very difficult to find a suitable place, particularly on a major event like the RAC Rally. On this event, it is not at all unusual for cars to be parked on both sides of an access road for two miles either side of a stage. Some spectators will have walked very much further! These people will be there before your service crew, and the place they take will be the place your service car would have liked to use.

Always keep one car back at the start, particularly if the rally car has been kept in the open in cold weather. Although you are usually

Service-point reconnaissance before the RAC Rally. Knowing exactly where to expect a service car can sometimes save retirement

It's always a relief to find your service crew where you expect them to be. (Shekhar Mehta and Martin, 1974 San Remo Rally, Lancia Beta Coupé)

allowed to push a car out of a *parc fermé*, you must usually have the engine running at time controls.

Be clear about servicing rules – and make certain the crews are as well. Some rallies are very well ordered; some, sadly including our own RAC Rally, have a history of leaving people uncertain about exactly what should be done. I prepare a service schedule, using carbon paper so I have a duplicate copy of the instructions given to the crews. Few things upset a driver more, on the moment of discovery, than a missing service point. You are always the first object of suspicion. 'Where should it be? Why don't you know? Didn't you bother to check the points with the crew? How far do you expect me to drive on this puncture?' Once you have experienced this sort of situation you will know what I mean! Change of service plans are always fraught with possible errors. This may occur because a team-mate of yours has had to retire, maybe because the route has been altered. After a long time in a rally car, the mental effort of concentrating on the details of a service crew plan is something you can do without. The only trouble is that the original plan was probably your work of art, and nobody else knows what overall plan you were trying to fulfil.

Petrol and tyres

One of your most important responsibilities is controlling the amount of petrol in the rally car. Different factors affect your choice. Some cars accelerate better with a half-tank or so than a near-empty tank, simply because the extra weight gives better traction. Remember the different rates of consumption between stages and road sections – and between top-gear flat-out tests and narrow second-gear ones. Always play for safety: Chris and I usually calculate accurately for each point, and then add two gallons for luck. We calculate how much petrol must be in the tank, not how much must be added. Often because of a long road section we still have more than the minimum specified, so none need be added. The extra two gallons might just help if a service crew cannot reach a point . . .

The next most important decision must be that you have the correct tyres ready. There are some wrong conceptions. It is seldom fatal to tackle a stage on the wrong tyres, and certainly not on short stages. Even racing tyres can be driven hard over rocky ground without deflating. The longer the stage, the more important is the choice. Judging weather conditions is an art. Never rush ahead to tackle a snowy test: usually it is best to tackle it late, if you have the opportunity to hang back.

On the 1971 RAC Rally we drove along without haste in Scotland during a spell of bad weather, and to our surprise we found we were at the start of a stage before anyone else. In the darkness we had thought we had seen various spectators' cars parked beside the route before the stage; only later did we realize they weren't spectators – they were other drivers waiting for us to arrive first!

The driver is always the final decision-maker about tyres, but it is up to you, when you have a choice, to arrange the service car schedules so that you can give yourself that choice when you need it. Always remember that the highest stages are the ones where really bad weather is most likely. A driver will always expect you to have a good idea of surfaces of stages in advance. If it is a secret route event, go and ask an organizer if you do not know. Most will tell you: if they do not, it is usually because they want it to be a surprise – so be prepared accordingly.

		⋮		SS 33 Broxa 2 Finish
		R.C.C. ↑		R.C.C. 9
	00.00	⊤		Leave Stage
0.70	0.70	✕	(A)	
1.55	2.25	⊤→	(B)	
1.08	3.33	∠	(C)	Whitby
1.58	4.91	⊤	(D)	
0.61	5.52	⊣		Enter Stage

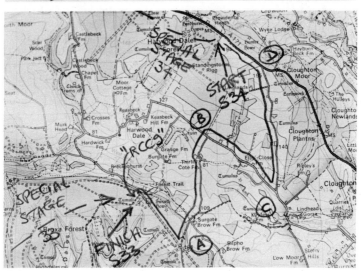

These pictures show how to mark a map from a Tulip style route instruction. The letters represent the various points at which a driver has to make a turning

The tripmeter

On road sections where you have Tulip signs, take care to tick off the junctions whenever you zero the tripmeter. Every now and again you will forget to zero the meter, and if you tick the instruction in your road book nonetheless you will soon be lost! It may be that you have a second meter for overall readings but by the time there have been some minor route changes, or a new roundabout, and again by the time you have changed tyres and thrown your meter out of adjustment, the overall reading will be suspect. Incidentally, if you use a Halda Twin-master, always use the lower meter for junction-to-junction readings and the top one for overall readings. It is possible to adjust the top

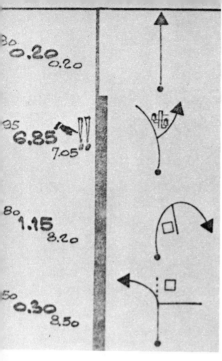

The instruction at interim distance 6.85 as shown on the route instructions and as seen by the driver on the road

Space-age trip meter and rally clocks

reading (or both readings) but not the bottom one alone. Particularly if you have to stretch to reach the meter, it is easily possible to pull the wrong lever. Some flexible tubing attached to a lever immediately ensures that you pull that lever rather than the other one. One of the biggest troubles with Halda meters is the reflections from the glass. Light coming through the rear window causes reflections, while the illuminating lamp inside the meter causes internal reflections at night. Some people disconnect this lamp and mount a bulb shining from the outside, to eliminate the latter problem. As for the former trouble, this is usually corrected by tilting the meter till the reflection is eliminated.

The co-driver as driver

Co-driving is not just a name for sitting in the passenger seat checking the timekeepers' watches: it can often mean just what it says. Despite the satisfaction of being able to drive distances unaided, in general a tired rally driver is a bad rally driver, so it is important that you should have the reputation of being a safe, smooth and reliable driver in your own right. Your driver will always tell you if he does not want you to drive, but before calling upon him for a decision tell him how much longer he will have to continue driving if he does not take the immediate opportunity to rest. You do not want to have to drive on a section which is difficult navigationally, even if the roads are good and the time schedule easy. If a section is easy enough for you to be able to take over the driving it must also be easy enough for him to drive and do the navigating himself – so if he does not want you to drive, you should try to rest instead. Even though the driver needs split-second judgement more than you, even when you have pace notes to read, you need to conserve your energy as best as you can. Your job will continue after you reach the finish, when the results are being displayed – and if there is any discussion about the results to be done, you will need every ounce of energy you can muster. When you are practising for a training rally, drive from time to time so that your driver can understand how you drive and maybe correct your style to his preference. The reduction of energy consumption within a rally car is of great importance. Anxiety is a major cause of energy expenditure. In everything you do, think how to attain your objective without unnecessary exertion.

Stages

The stages are the major points on rallies, and everything you do should be geared to enabling your driver to attain the best times he can, not just on one or some of the stages, but on the aggregate as well. Checking times is the most obvious chore for you to handle: even on the biggest rallies times can be mistaken by the marshals. If you gain a minute in this way, the organizers are likely to spot the error and correct it, but if you lose a minute, it is up to you to correct the error when it arises. Otherwise you will need to embark on a very convincing argument to establish that you did not skid off the road for that minute! More stage rallies are lost by co-drivers missing a minute-error than by any other single cause.

On secret route rallies it is always debatable how much more a co-driver can usefully do. I make it my business to know as much as I can about a stage, particularly where the really bad corners lie, and also from time to time where the flat crests lie. Certainly knowledge of bad bends will usually slow down a driver, particularly on a forest event, but it also leads to safer rallying, and before you win you must first finish. Sometimes even the most dangerous bends are not cautioned, or the warning boards are knocked down by an earlier car.

The difficulty of course is that you can only learn about stages by entering other rallies, and you cannot make notes about them because this would infringe the 'no-notes' rules. Ordnance Survey maps sometimes show stage-roads on maps, with their bends, but there are so many other hazards which are not marked that reliance on these maps is of little overall benefit. It is probably more useful to a driver if you call out the angles of arrows in the distance. A driver focuses his eyes in the middle distance, and although he can often sense the presence of

If you have your window open on stages, make certain things do not fly out!

93

an approaching arrow he will have to change the focus of his eyes to look up at it. You can save this distraction by telling him what the arrow says. Avoid all other distractions. Never say something that is not important. Even on secret route events, the use of intercoms is an advantage simply because the driver needs to make less effort to understand what you say.

Always try to identify stages with names and characteristics. The first time you enter a stage event, names are very confusing. I can think of three Park Farm special stages in use on special stage events, and your first sortie into the forests of Wales will bring mental collapse if you even try to pronounce Coed-y-Brenin or Myherin, let alone attempt to work out individualities. But they do have individual characteristics and identifying certain features leads to future understanding. As a starter, most of the Clocaenog stages we regard as being pretty 'fail-safe', but the opposite is the case of the Coed-y-Brenin complex. There are two or three distinct fire-breaks in that area alone. All you, as a co-driver, can constructively do is to make a driver aware of where he is. Something which many clubmen never appreciate is that they will probably have a far better knowledge of many stages than the professional teams. When the Army ranges at Eppynt were regularly used on the RAC Rally, for example, club drivers were always among those with the best times. Stage rallying, generally, is a matter of confidence. This knowledge of characteristics of stages helps by injecting confidence; but the nature of forest stages in particular is so variable that actual knowledge, unless very recent, seldom benefits much.

Changing a wheel

Chris has mentioned elsewhere planning how to carry out wheel changes. Should you have a puncture: before making the decision about stopping, a driver will always want to know exactly how much further it is to the end of the stage. Once again, you can throw the ultimate decision on to him, but make certain your information is correct. If you have failed to zero the tripmeter at the start, as a last resort you can see from your stopwatch how long you have been driving and in this way gain some idea of how much further down the stage you have to go. Tell him what you know, never guess without saying that you are doing so.

Having to change wheels is fortunately not a frequent occurrence, but when it happens it is not the end of the world. Far worse is retirement through taking a rash decision to press on with a puncture. Shekhar Mehta and I once drove to the end of a Kielder stage with a puncture, only to suffer a wheel breakage and suspension collapse. We nearly died of exposure in that forest. When eventually you get going again, systematically sort out the car. Unless he is not concerned, try to do up the driver's belts, then do up yours and if your hands are dirty clean them as best you can before making any of your paperwork dirty. And however disturbed your routine, never forget to check that time at the end of the stage!

Penalties

Calculate your total penalties as you go along, taking care to note individual penalties before cards are handed in. When interim penalties are announced, they will be based on the totals at certain earlier card-collection points, so be ready to compare your total points at the place concerned with the penalties of leading competitors. Sometimes you never know the official times, particularly on certain foreign events, and so your only chance to see how you are doing is by noting your stop-watch times. Strangely the secrecy of this system often leads to greater accuracy than the British method of inviting competitors to check times for themselves.

Do not get fussed about stage times in the early stages of a long event: it is the position at the finish that really matters. I never know what to do when well-meaning rivals come and ask me for stage times. Certainly it is nice when they disclose their own times, but it is often very tempting to throw in one or two fictitious times just to see if a rival will ease off unnecessarily. Would this be sporting? I do not know. What is sporting behaviour? I often think it is behaviour to which you would not object if the other man did it to you. It will differ from case to case. On road events, for instance, it might be good sport to hustle a marshal into reading his watch wrongly so that you gain a minute or two, but if you did this on a stage event it would simply cause havoc and possibly lead to the stage being cancelled through uncertainty.

Checking results

The end of the rally is your particular moment of truth. If missing a wrong minute is the greatest cause of losing a stage rally, the second most common is the co-driver missing a material error in the results. One of the home Internationals was once won by the wrong driver. The day after the results were finalized and results distributed, it was discovered that the wrong man had won. Too late. Final. One of your most important functions is to check results at the right time.

The regulations often specify on multi-day events that results can only be queried on that day. Afterwards they are final even though the rally itself goes on. This is hard work for a co-driver; in the early stages he will not only have to check times of rivals but also of other people who ultimately are due to retire or suffer heavy penalties later on. Easy for the organizers but a bad burden for the competitor. Your job is to make certain the results are right. It is not to explore pernickety complaints, to seek cancellations of stages when you personally were not inconvenienced. On the other hand, your job does not allow you to relax your vigil until you know everything is correct. It is very dangerous to think that you have a sufficient margin not to call for further corrections: you do not know what corrections your rival is calling for at that moment. Find out where results will be published, and if you are likely to be elsewhere make certain you are told immediately when they are published. Know how to process a protest, know also your

You do your job and let your driver do his! (Marc and Christine Etchebers, 1975 Spanish Rally)

rights of appeal. Be prepared to implement these; command of the rules establishes you as a contender worthy of serious treatment. Less worthy contenders will hedge at such a point: if this is their reaction, how sure are they of their grounds in the first place? A protest is generally a sign that you have failed in your art of friendly persuasion! If a matter arises that carries no precedent and the organizers cannot handle it fairly, have no qualms about calling for a decision from higher authority. It is not the job of an organizer to create fresh precedents in relation to interpretation of rules. You owe it to the sport to have unresolved problems ironed out so that others know another time what should be done.

When the results are final, then at last you can ease your attention. Not too much, lest you oversleep and miss the prize-giving and insult your hosts; not too much in case you do not have time to tell your tale of glory (or woe) to the gentlemen of the Press so that you miss the chance of a mention in the papers next week; not too much in case you fail to claim your trade bonuses within the time required. It seems that a co-driver's work is never done.

10 *Foreign rallies*
By CHRIS SCLATER

The endurance aspect of British rallies is fast disappearing. The ultra-reliable car with mediocre performance can no longer expect to achieve results. The pressure of tight timing schedules has lifted, mainly out of necessity. For the sport to survive in the UK, the press-on-regardless attitude of past years must go. Because of the trend toward easy road timing and the resulting ability of service teams to carry out remarkable mechanical repairs, the winning car is normally the fastest.

Abroad the changes are coming more slowly. Police attitudes toward rallies are hardening, in order to appease public opinion. But tight schedules, and with them the need for endurance qualities from both car and driver, still apply. I find that competing in a foreign event is real rallying. More demands are put on the whole team, and as well as driving skill, ingenuity and experience play a much larger part.

As discussed in an earlier chapter, the majority of continental events are on known roads. Practising is allowed and the majority of entrants will use pace notes. There are exceptions however, the most notable being the Swedish Rally which reverted to secret route in 1976. The Total Rally in South Africa is traditionally secret, as is the Southern Cross in Australia and the Rideau Lakes in Canada. All the Finnish events are secret except for their premier rally, the Thousand Lakes, which is a counter to the World Rally Championship.

The very fact that you have to make pace notes puts up the cost of competing considerably. A recce car or practice car has to be used. Most private entrants will only use a recce car, which, as its description implies, is a standard car used simply to drive slowly over the route. Works teams will invariably use practice cars which are replica rally cars. This gives them the tremendous advantage of being able to drive at rally speeds over the route and therefore perfect their pace notes to a far higher degree than a privateer could hope for.

In addition to the transportation costs for an extra vehicle or the cost of hiring a car on the spot, the accompanying expenses build up. Insurance and petrol for the car, and hotel expenses to cover two people for up to a month – in the case of an event like the Monte Carlo or Moroccan Rallies – have to be faced.

In a number of cases rally organizers are willing to assist foreign competitors. The Acropolis Rally in Greece offers a cash payment to help defray travelling expenses. A number of Spanish rallies will help to subsidize hotel bills and help to arrange special rates on boat fares.

The 1974 Total Rally in South Africa – traditionally a secret route rally (Chris, in second place)

The preparation for a foreign rally starts months before. One of the first decisions to take is that of a co-driver – if you're able to find one who can spare the time to compete abroad. There are few co-drivers in a position to take weeks off work for sorties abroad. Their holidays are probably geared up for British rallying. Those professionals who are available will cost you money because it is their livelihood. They may not always want a fee, but will certainly want every penny of their expenses paid. The final factor in your choice of co-drivers must be their experience – in particular experience in the use of pace notes. Certainly if you – as a driver – have never used notes before, a partner with experience in that field is essential.

The next thing is to contact the rally organizers. Get a copy of the regulations and the route and find out what concessions they can offer – you may even be able to get a free entry, a considerable saving. The possibility of cheap boat tickets should also be investigated.

You are nearly in a position to draw up a budget. The final unknown expenses may be the cost of a mechanic, or mechanics. One service car is normally adequate at this level and if you don't have friends willing

The finish of the 1973 Firestone Rally – an event which is pleased to have British competitors

Chris Sclater finishes in the Acropolis Rally

to service at their own expense, you may have to pay a mechanic. The cost of participation for the Firestone, a typical European championship rally in northern Spain, based on 1975 figures, would be as follows:

Equipment:
1 recce car travelling cross-channel to France, then driving to Spain
1 service car and trailer, with rally car, boat to northern Spain
Personnel
2 mechanics, plus 1 driver, plus 1 co-driver

Mechanics' wages	£100.00
Boat tickets	170.00
Green card insurance	35.00
RAC medical insurance	7.50
Total petrol expenses	195.00
Hotel expenses	200.00
	£707.50

This covers four or five days recce, but does not include the cost of tyres which obviously will vary depending on car and discount you may be able to obtain.

The one last problem which has to be overcome is that of temporary importation of spare parts. An ATA carnet is accepted and understood everywhere in Europe and in almost every country in the world. This is a document which, in effect, is a guarantee issued by the Chamber of Commerce in London that duty will be paid if you fail to re-export the goods from a foreign country within a given time limit. A deposit has to be paid to the Chamber of Commerce and is a percentage of the value of the goods. This could be covered by a bank guarantee which you would have to arrange yourself.

For a rally team a carnet can be a two-edged sword as I have discovered. It is a tremendous help for speedy travel through customs formalities, so long as the man dealing with carnets is not at lunch. But if you fail to get the correct page stamped at a border, especially if you are leaving a foreign country, the penalties can be severe and non-refundable.

I have driven on the Portuguese Rally many times and in 1971 there was a long run from London across France and Spain into Portugal at a remote country crossing. There was a customs post, but at nine in the morning the man officiating hardly knew what a passport was – let alone a carnet. My service car had followed on the rally route in case of problems and crossed at the same place. Needless to say they didn't manage to get the carnet stamped. The result was a demand from the Spanish authorities, via the London Chamber of Commerce, for £300. I had to pay or go to court. I explained the circumstances and, because this was a relatively trivial offence, received a refund about eighteen months later. But it was touch and go and ever since I have been a bit frightened of carnets!

Of course this organization for a rally is not vital. It may be important for success, but to begin with, anyway, you are going to compete abroad for fun and to see how things are done. I remember my first foreign rally very well. It was the *Coupe des Alpes* in 1969. Talk about jumping in at the deep end! It was the first event in the Escort TC I had bought from Fords. Hywel Thomas was my co-driver and he arranged for two friends to service at their own expense in their own road car. In addition, I had the promise of assistance from Fords where they could help. We drove the rally car down overnight and started to recce straight away – in the rally car. After a couple of days we met up with Roger Clark and Jim Porter who'd finished their recce. They were kind enough to lend us their car so we could leave the rally car in a garage at Marseilles, the starting town.

I had managed to persuade Castrol to part with £100 for petrol expenses, and Dunlop had offered me a set of racing tyres. John Davenport had lent me Ove Andersson's pace notes to copy. So, one way or another, we were more or less organized. One slight embarrassment was our starting number. It was 35, and Ove Andersson in the third works Escort was down at 70, nearly one hour behind the other members of the Ford works team. In the circumstances I was bound to offer a swap, on the basis of 'one favour deserves another', and Stuart Turner made the necessary arrangements.

Bob de Jong and Chris on the Boucles de Spa *rally in Belgium – a relatively cheap foreign event to enter*

It can be very cold in Scandinavia in winter! Martin's Polski-Fiat is rescued during the Arctic Rally

Several things struck me about that first sortie abroad. The atmosphere was very exciting, with crowds of people lining the public roads, treating the drivers more like gladiators or bull-fighters. The whole concept of using public roads which were closed to other traffic was fascinating. Even between stages the roads were closed to other traffic, because of the very high average speeds that were set. The pressure was on constantly and, in fact, the Alpine Coupe for remaining unpenalized on the road timing was a very difficult prize to win. The other thing that amazed me was the sight of black lines left by a sliding Alpine to within inches of a five-hundred foot drop on the Col d'Allos.

My rally ended after a day, when I hit a bridge parapet on a narrow stage near Entrevaux. But I had done enough to realize the appeal that continental events provided. I decided to compete abroad as much as possible.

My next expedition was to Sweden in January 1970 for the Swedish Rally. A totally different scene from the Alpine. The racing tyres were substituted by studded snow tyres and instead of clothes for a Mediterranean summer we needed protection from −30 degrees centigrade cold.

Fords were doing the Swedish as well, and with their assistance in the way of service added to my sponsorship from the British branch of the Jolly Club and Goodyear tyres, we were all set once more. I hadn't bargained for the very high cost of living in Sweden and when other crews were eating in the hotel on their expense money, co-driver Peter Valentine and I slipped over the road for a cheaper meal in the self-service café!

It was so cold that if you couldn't get your car into a heated garage, it was best to leave it running all day! I left mine out the first night we were there and it took a mile of clutch-slipping on the end of a tow rope to persuade the engine and gearbox to revolve. The oil was so cold it was like glue. The battery efficiency is halved at that sort of temperature as well.

Although it would have been possible to recce the route, we didn't have time for more than a couple of days. One of these days I spent driving round a circuit on a frozen lake to get used to ice driving. The other was spent in the back of Simo Lampinen's road-going Saab as he checked his pace notes on some of the stages. In fact, he was taking John Davenport on the rally and once more we benefited from him with a copy of his pace notes. I might add that Simo drove a lot quicker in his road car than I ever did on the rally!

Essential equipment on a snow rally includes two shovels. And we needed them. We had to dig ourselves out of snowbanks three times and the fourth time the car was too far off to have any chance of staying in the event. But I had driven nearly half the stages and had learnt an enormous amount. It was a bit demoralizing to be overtaken by Group One cars after only a few kilometres on a stage and really I had to teach myself very quickly – or lose face!

Clearly on these early events I had been lucky with the sort of help I received. It was not always going to be like that. There would be times when Fords would not be on the same event and times when Davenport's pace notes wouldn't be available. But by now I was able to be more independent anyway. In 1970 I formed an association with J.C.Withers (Winsford) Ltd, a car-breaking company in Cheshire who were involved in the sale of spares for rally cars. They part-sponsored me, but I still drove and prepared my own car.

The first rally I did with Withers' assistance was the Circuit of Ireland in 1970. Second place behind Roger Clark was a good start to

Successful debut with J. C. Withers: Chris in second place on the 1970 Circuit of Ireland in an ex-works Escort

any association and since the whole entry was a low-key level, everyone was very pleased. In fact, this turned out to be one of my most successful years in rallying. Second on the Welsh and victory on the Manx followed the Circuit.

Flushed with success, the idea of competing on the Sherry Rally in Spain was appealing. The British Leyland team had entered with two Minis but because of a withdrawal from motor sport they cancelled the entries at the last moment. This meant that there were two co-drivers available with knowledge of the route, because they had already done a preliminary recce. One of these was Tony Nash – Paddy Hopkirk's man at the time. I phoned him and he agreed to do the event with me. The start was in Madrid. I took the rally car (another Escort TC bought from Fords) on the boat to Bilbao and drove to Madrid. Tony Nash flew down and met me there. We hired a SEAT 1430 and recced the route – making pace notes for all the stages. Most of these were uphill and all on tarmac. Apparently the Spaniards didn't like the loose or downhill. After problems with two hire cars and a stint of pace-noting from the back seat of a taxi, we eventually finished the recce and made our way back to Madrid. Our service crew was none other than Tony Mason, who was later to work at Ford Competitions Department as Rallies Liaison Officer, and Ian Harwood, who was Cal Withers' assistant at the time.

They flew down and used our recce as a service car. The spares I had brought with me were transferred from the rally car, and once more we were all set for an attempt at success abroad. Unfortunately the engine failed at half-way when we were in third place.

The Portuguese Rally was the next trip and this time I took Mike Wood, a well-known ex-BMC co-driver. It was more a case of his taking me in fact. We had a rather hurried recce, but Mike taught me a lot about the preparation for a rally of this type. In those days the Portuguese, or the TAP as it was known, because of the airline sponsorship, was a very difficult rally. Ten finishers was the average. The big problem was to lose as little time on the road sections as possible. Some of them were impossible at any speed, and some were just about on. Very few were easy.

Because the distances on the road book tended to be shorter than those actually covered, it was difficult to assess how hard you had to drive 'on the night'. To make certain, we made pace notes on the majority of the road sections as well as the special stages. At the end of the recce – having checked distances – we knew where things would be tight, and where they would be very tight.

Unfortunately we had water pump failure at exactly half distance, but again I had learnt a tremendous amount. The Portuguese is now a round in the World Championship, and is a classic of its kind. It is one of the few events where the police encourage rally cars to go faster and speed limits are effectively ignored. The atmosphere is more like that of a bull-fight than a rally.

Making pace notes for a road section may seem very strange, and it would certainly be easy not to bother, especially if you're tired and

TAP Rally in Portugal, 1972

hungry and keen to find a hotel. But the worst eventualities must be considered. There are certain roads where you might drive no faster with unchecked notes than you would with none at all. However, you must consider the possibility of fog, ice or snow – or perhaps a mechanical failure on the car which could be repaired more quickly if the route to the service point is known. Certainly note-making is a very tiring business, mentally, but an essential skill to master.

My first professional entry in a continental event was the Monte Carlo in 1973. I had won the Kleber Wheelbase Scholarship in December 1972 and the first event for the Escort that was the prize was the Monte. John Davenport was co-driving and we were the third members of the Ford team, getting full works service together with tyre service from Kleber in Europe. We recced the route with a hired Simca and, having done the rally once before and been involved with other factory participation in previous years, my knowledge of the event was quite thorough.

I still think that of all the rallies I have done the Monte is the biggest challenge, to the driver anyway. The one let-down is the long 'run in' from the various starting points in Europe, which all converge in Monaco where the real action begins. We started from Glasgow and the two-thousand kilometre drive to the Principality was very tedious and tiring. The remainder of the event is completely different. There are two competitive loops into the mountains – one of thirty hours and another of twelve. Each has a number of special stages, but really the pressure is on all the time. Tyres have to be changed at every special stage, as well as petrol taken and a checkover made on the car – not to mention curing any mechanical problems there may be. And all this at an average speed of about sixty kilometres an hour. The other small problem is the police and their radar traps!

We didn't lose any time at the time controls but there were a few **105** occasions when it was a close-run thing, such as just scraping in with a few seconds to spare after a wheel change. During the whole event we used ninety-five tyres, not actually worn out but used and then changed. The conditions on the Monte can vary from smooth, dry tarmac through patchy ice to packed snow – or even blizzard conditions. In order to make the correct choice of tyre for each special stage the factory teams have 'ice-note crews' who have checked conditions before the rally cars arrive and can advise the drivers.

The idea is to have a tyre for every condition available at the start of every stage. In our case, with Kleber, we had three different types of tyre. A racing tyre for dry tarmac, a mud and snow with about two hundred and fifty studs for ice or hard-packed snow, and a narrow snow tyre with about six hundred studs for deep snow. The other Ford cars, who were using Dunlop, had about five or six choices available to them, so you can see it isn't very difficult to use ninety-five tyres.

The current regulations are restricting the choice of tyres and the number of studs. They change nearly every week but in 1976 the Monte organizers required the same tread pattern to be used throughout the event. It was possible to vary the number of studs. Certainly restricting the choice of tyres is a good thing on grounds of expense alone, but unfortunately the Monte is known for slightly strange rules and regulations (such as those leading to the Mini headlight disqualification) and the situation is not very satisfactory. But this doesn't detract from the actual driving challenge which confronts the crews.

After the thirty-hour loop, which in 1973 was almost totally in heavy snow conditions, we arrived back in Monte ready for a day and a half's rest before the complementary test – or twelve-hour mountain circuit, as it is known. This is effectively a flat-out run over about seven hundred kilometres on the night of Thursday/Friday, covering usually seven to nine special stages. The famous Col de Turini is used three times and the Col de Couillole (sometimes called St Sauveur) twice. The first and last test is a normally dry, twisty tarmac loop, not far from Monte, called Peille. It's run in both directions and is invariably dry, allowing the use of racing tyres. In 1973 the other stages were of mixed conditions. Both the Turini and the Couillole were half snow and half dry tarmac. For these five tests we opted for the 250 studded mud and snow tyres. This proved to be the right choice and had the added advantage of cutting down tyre service problems by allowing us to do tests 2 to 6 on the same type of tyre, although probably not the same set.

That last night was unforgettable. I didn't have time to get tired and the most marvellous feeling of all was reaching the last hill before the drop down into Monaco and the finish – and watching the sunrise reflecting off the Mediterranean Sea. A complete contrast to the high snowbanks on the Turini covered by thousands of people huddled round wood fires, and the sheet ice on the descent of the Couillole where speeds of 160 kilometres an hour are reached. The atmosphere can be felt everywhere and particularly at the service points. The mechanics are fantastic – their sheer enthusiasm is a tonic in itself and the support of the large crowds makes you realize how special the

Monte Carlo Rally is. With Hannu Mikkola 4th, Makinen 11th and myself 16th, Ford won the team prize. It was probably my most enjoyable rally and certainly the one that taught me most about professionalism in both the preparation and actual competition of a major international event.

The thirty-hour mountain section on the Monte, together with the very tiring thirty-six hour first half of the Acropolis, and I'm sure the Safari (although I haven't competed in East Africa), highlight the different physical effects of foreign events from the British. Certainly the man who can remain physically fitter than the next will succeed in these events. In addition, there is a smaller proportion of ultra-competitive machinery to compete against abroad, and, for this reason alone, the challenge is worth taking up. The other attraction is prize money. Although British prize money is improving – notably in the Irish events – there is more to be won outside our shores. Although expenses have to be covered, it is still possible to make money through reliability and good preparation. It's always said that a British driver prepared to live in Spain for six months could clean up and come home with a small pot of gold. I'm sure that's true – and I would be keen to prove it!

The atmosphere of the Monte is summed up by this picture of the Turini Test

11 *Confidence*
By MARTIN HOLMES

Co-drivers are on a hiding to nothing. When their schemes work well and take drivers to victory, the co-drivers must stand patiently in the background like servants waiting for the applause for their drivers to die down. If their schemes fail, you can be certain that the co-driver will be number one scapegoat. The greatest satisfaction that a co-driver can expect is to be told by a driver that his efforts were appreciated. Never expect anything more! How you react to the occasions which will surely come when you are the most-hated co-driver in the world is important. My luck has often enabled me to escape from disaster by a hair's-breadth, but I can recall two ghastly occasions when it did not.

The Mintex International Rally started its life as a fabulous event known as the Seven Dales, and this was the final event in the national RAC series ever to include competitive road sections. It gave people like me who did a lot of road rallying the chance to enjoy full-blooded stage rallying in addition to a good night's sport 'in the lanes'. Perhaps even more satisfying, people like us were in demand for once! Tony Mason was invited to navigate Roger Clark on the event in question, and Chris had asked me long before the event to keep the date free. I had longed to win the Seven Dales. The year before, Tony Fowkes and I had crashed only three sections from the finish when in the lead, and nobody had given us a second thought as a possible winner. Chris had a far more powerful car and with the exception of Clark there was nobody who had as much all-round experience in rallying as we did. We desperately wanted to win. In fact, Clark was uncatchable, so the best we could have achieved was second place, but it was my fault that we didn't.

At whatever your level of rallying, there is always a reason why you make a mistake: sometimes there are dozens of factors which contribute to that awful final error. This time there were plenty! It all started a couple of minutes before the start, when Keith Wood, a rival from the road rallying, had warned me that part of the road sections later that night were around the new M6 motorway workings, and that there were changes to the map. He agreed to explain the exact details when we met later at a time control, so I thought no further about the problem for the moment. We had a full day of stage rallying to think about before then! I was a little puzzled that I did not see Keith at all

Chris and Martin on the ill-fated 1972 Seven Dales Rally – before road sections were outlawed from nationals, before intercoms became universal, and before there was a limit on the number of auxiliary lights which can be used on road sections (1.8 litre RS 1600)

after that conversation at the start, but did not worry unduly, since he had always been the sort of chap who did not forget a promise, and anyway there were the immediate problems of the rally to think about . . .

Then we broke our exhaust pipe. This is a far more dangerous hazard than you might think, for often the fumes seep into the car and dull your reactions. Mine became well and truly blurred on this occasion. When you have co-driven or navigated for long enough you achieve the ability to do things automatically, and this can even extend to map-reading. For several hours, I had little idea what I was doing (this time I admit it!) except I remember wandering off at every service point to get as much fresh air as I could. At times like these, your best-laid plans start to go wrong. Our 'best-laid' plan was to have a friend, Peter Moss, ready to explore certain portions of the route that might be ambiguous from the instructions, or possibly explore a stretch of road that was obviously not intended to be part of the rally route but which might be usable and which consequently might save penalties if that section proved to be tight on time. Still, I had Keith's promise in my mind, and as I had other queries for Peter to resolve, I sent him off to deal with these rather than the query that ultimately proved to be our downfall. Then I heard that Keith had retired at the very starting-ramp, with a broken engine, which was why I had not seen him since. By now, Peter had left on his errands.

I still do not know how we covered the road sections. Most of them used long, hard routes, and to our disgrace we had Clark catching us up on most of them. This gave us the feeling that we must be doing very badly, which added to the general feeling of gloom. Whenever I had a conscious moment over and above the attentions demanded by the maps, my mind kept wandering to the questions of that junction. We were given little explanatory diagrams whenever the maps were out of date. These were not to scale, but at least they were sufficient. Then we arrived at the place concerned. 'It's tricky,' were Keith's last words to me. I took the less obvious turning and travelled what seemed to be the correct distance to the place where the next control should be. Any mental haze that had been hanging over the navigator suddenly cleared away. I came face to face with an ugly truth. I was well off-route. In the end we reached the control about five minutes late, sufficient even on an event of some eighteen hours to drop us from second to fifth position. The correct turning had been the obvious one, though road works in the vicinity would have certainly been sufficient to cause a navigator some alarm had they not been known about in advance. What had gone wrong? I had tried to make a simple situation too difficult, and with other things distracting me, I had stopped appreciating exactly what was happening. It was also one of those times when I wanted something so badly that I stopped myself achieving it.

The other horrible nightmare occurred three years later, again with Chris. The Sherry Rally in 1975 was the first Sherry Rally when things really seemed to go well for the organizers. Every previous year the rally had been spoiled because things went wrong for the organizers, or the organizers did things that were odd compared with other events. The rally had always enjoyed fabulous stages but these were not everything. You had to get everything else right as well! You had to avoid the radar traps, you had to know all the rules and read the small print carefully. The year before, the man who had won had only finished third overall on stage times!

Chris and Martin tackle the final stage on the 1975 Sherry Rally with David Sutton's Group 2 RS 2000

1) TIME SCHEDULE

Closing date for applications: 9th september at 20.00 hours at the Automobile Club of Jerez.
— To obtain documents: :17th september between 8 and 12 hours at the Automobile Club of Jerez.
— Scrutineering: 17th september 1975 in Park Ferme situated in the gardens of El Bosque in the pak Gonzales Hontoria, Paseo de Las Palmeras.
  Hours:
  a) Nos. 1 to 30 - from 09 to 11 hours
  b) Nos. 31 to 60 - from 11 to 13 hours
  c) Nos. 61 onwards - from 13 to 15 hours
  d) For vehicles which have been refused and which may be corrected - from 16 to 17 hours.

NOTA. Competitors must present themselves together with their vehicles at the Park Ferme, at least 30 minutes before the latest hour corresponding to their assigned number.

— Publishing of the scrutineered vehicles: In the Automobile Club at 20.00 hours on 17th september.
— Start of the Rally for the first car: On the 18th september at 00.01 hours.
— Arrival of first competitor at Park Ferme in Ronda: (At end of the first section) 18th september at 09.10 hours.
— De parture of first competitor from the Park Ferme in Ronda: 18th september at 13.01 hours.
— Arrival of first competitor at Park Ferme in Puerto Banus (end of the second section and first stage): 19th september at 05.00 hours.
— Departure of first competitor from the Park Fermé in Puerto Banus 19th september at 14.01 hours.
— Arrival of first competitor at Park Fermé in Ronda: (End of the third section): 20th september at 03.24 hours.
— Departure of first competitor from the Park Fermé in Ronda: 20th september at 07.01 hours.
— Arrival of first competitor at Open Park in Puerto de Santa Maria (Motel Caballo Blanco): 20th september at 11.01 hours.
— Departure of first competitor from the Open Park in Puerto de Santa Maria: 20 september at 13.01 hours.
— Arrival of first competitor at Park Fermé in Jerez de la Frontera. (End of fourth section, second stage and Rally): 20th september at 13.46 hours.
— Publishing of Results: 20th september at 19.00 hours in the Automobile Club of Jerez.
— Prizegiving: 20th september at 22 hours at the Palace of Wine.

1) HORARIOS

— Cierre de inscripciones: El día 9 de septiembre de 1975, a las 20 horas en la sede social del Automóvil Club de Jerez.
— Entrega de Documentaciones: El día 17 de septiembre de 1975, en los locales del Automóvil Club de Jerez, entre las 8 y 12 horas.
— Verificaciones: El día 17 de septiembre de 1975 en el Parque Cerrado en Jerez, sito junto al Restaurante «El Bosque» del Parque González Hontoria.

a) Números 1 al 30: desde las 9 a las 11 horas.
b) Números 31 al 60: desde las 11 a las 13 horas.
c) Números 61 al final: desde las 13 a las 15 horas.
d) Los que hayan sido rechazados por alguna causa corregible: desde las 16 a las 17 horas.
NOTA.— Los participantes deberán presentarse en el Parque Cerrado al menos 30 minutos antes de la hora tope que les corresponde por su número.

— Publicación de la lista de verificados: En el Automóvil Club a las 20 horas del día 17.
— Salida del 1.er participante del Parque Cerrado en Jerez: El día 18 de septiembre a las 00.01 horas.
— Llegada del 1.er participante al Parque Cerrado en Ronda: (Fin del 1.er Sector): Día 18 de septiembre a las 09.10 horas.
— Salida 1.er participante del Parque Cerrado de Ronda: Día 18 de septiembre a las 13.01.
— Llegada del 1.er participante al Parque Cerrado en Puerto Banús (Fin del 2.º Sector y 1.ª Etapa): Día 19 de septiembre a las 05.00 horas.
— Salida 1.er participante del Parque Cerrado en Puerto Banús: Día 19 de septiembre a las 14.01.
— Llegada del 1.er participante al Parque Cerrado en Ronda (Fin del 3.er Sector): Día 20 de septiembre a las 03.24 horas.

These pictures show why we were late for scrutineering!

It was my first Sherry Rally, and Chris kept warning me in advance to be careful all the time. But things seemed to be much better than expected. The organizers seemed to have only very minor troubles, even though we had been fined for reporting late at scrutineering. In the regulations there was a clause saying that you had to report for scrutineering at least thirty minutes before the end of your permitted times. Unfortunately in the English regulations this warning was given in small type – on another page. We were told that foreigners would have their fines returned. By all accounts the Sherry was reformed! By virtue of the Spanish habit of having accidents, most of the rival entries had retired and at the end of the final stage we were third behind the two professional SEAT team drivers.

Then they got me. We knew that we had a tight road section from the final stage to the finish, we knew that this would be tricky (we had found many small but distracting errors in the road block for this section), we were absolutely determined that we would complete this section on time, just as we had completed every other road section on the event. We went whistling through the complex maze of roads, not even hesitating at the places where the road block had been wrong, and we confidently ignored the instructions of a policeman who beckoned us the wrong way (our Escort RS2000 carried English registration plates). We did it all right and clocked in at the final control, on time. Then Canellas's co-driver pointed to an entry in our timecard under the 'neutralization' column. It said '+ 10', and was obviously intended to mean that we should take ten more minutes for that section. We had clocked in ten minutes early! This was another occasion when our number came up. Everything had been coincidental. I could not speak Spanish, so there was little point in the marshal trying to tell me the meaning of the entry in the column, as he had done for other competitors. Other competitors had an official delay on that section, which led to another entry in that column, so their attention was drawn to the original '+ 10' entry, later competitors on arriving at the control could see a queue of cars waiting before clocking in at the control and were warned that something was amiss. Every other entry in that column, earlier in the rally, had referred to an official delay rather than a change of time allowance.

Your first reaction at occasions such as these is bewilderment. You cannot accept that you are wrong. I think it is essential for any co-driver to believe in his own judgement, but the natural corollary of self-confidence is a refusal to accept that you are wrong. It is probably for this reason that most of the ugly scenes at the end of rallies when there are arguments to resolve are fought out between co-drivers. The aggrieved parties have made decisions which they believed to be correct at the time, and such is their self-confidence they cannot accept, even in the coolness of the morning afterwards, that they made the wrong decision at the time. I get terribly worked up about rallies. Success or failure becomes a very personal thing. Sometimes you are right, sometimes your wits carry you through a situation which should have been your downfall.

Many years ago one of the finest rallies in Britain was the Shunpiker. This represented the very best in road rallying in Wales in mid-winter, and it was rare among club events in using forests as well. It even had a gruelling race round Oulton Park at the end. It was a giant among the nationals. On this occasion I was navigating a friend with a 998 Cooper, a car which even as late as 1965 was capable of a place in the top ten of a national, if everything went right. On this occasion we had a complicated route that wound around the edges of the old maps 117,

The Shunpiker – a giant among national rallies in years gone by

127 and 128, and I made a mistake in plotting the route. I had failed to spot the road from Talerddig across to Dolgadfan and had taken the longer route using the A489 and B4518. There was a control at the crossroads two miles south of Llanbrynmair where the marshal told us we had approached from the wrong direction. Penalty, three hundred marks. In all innocence I said that this was not possible, since no direction of approach was specified. Ultimately I discovered that it had been, and that this had been completely missed earlier. The marshal was so taken by my genuine retort that he never marked the offence on the timecard and the error was never discovered. I am sure that this only happened because I was completely confident in what I was doing, even though it was wrong.

There is no harm in self-confidence, so long as you are adaptable and are able to understand immediately if circumstances have changed. Be quick to seize a good opportunity! On the 1975 RAC Rally Chris and I left the road on a special stage on the final night, in fact just six stages from the end. We were driving a Toyota Corolla which in addition to being a potential top-six car (Bjorn Waldegard had finished fourth the year before in such a car, and Chris was fifth when we went off the road) was also a dead-cert class winner. It was a long and miserable job getting the car back onto the road, even though it was undamaged. Unless, of course, the stage was going to be cancelled for some reason our hopes of a good place were dashed. It therefore simply became a matter of knowing when to stop our frantic work. The rules of that event stated that you had to arrive at the start of each special stage within one hour of scheduled time. As we had arrived at the start of this stage about twenty minutes down on scheduled time, and as the next stage followed almost immediately afterwards, we had only forty minutes before we were excluded from the rally. At moments such as this, when you are mentally exhausted as well as tired from disappointment and the physical effort of pushing the car, it is very easy to give up. All your driver wants to know is the moment when further effort is futile.

What saved the class win on this occasion was something quite beyond our control or command: in fact it was a combination of being in the right place at the right time and noticing relevant factors. The relevant factor was that no car had passed us as we were struggling with our rally car for a considerable period. We guessed that this was because there had been several cars off the road on this stage (we knew this from spectators' stories) and that the marshals had stopped the stage while they found out the extent of the carnage. In fact this never happened: there had been a complete blockage of cars outside the stage and for some twenty minutes no car could reach the start of the stage. Either way it seemed possible there would ultimately be an extension of overall time limit for this section. There had been such an extension at a previous control. The extension was likely to be for some round number of minutes (both previous extensions had been for thirty minutes) so we knew immediately that it was sensible to continue struggling with our car even though our forty minutes were passed.

The rest of the story is not relevant to this example, but briefly it was important for us not to instigate any application for an extension of time limit as we did not deserve it, but to find some other person who had a genuine cause for complaint and hope they were successful. In the end two such people came up and independently asked me how they could persuade the organizers to grant this extension, as they had both gone beyond maximum lateness because of this blockage. Eventually the organizers agreed and we took the benefit of this decision. The moral is, never be rigid in your decisions on how to handle a situation; always look for new approaches and see how they might help.

I had a fantastic example of good luck which at first looked like disaster earlier in 1975. Graham Lepley asked me to navigate on the Tour of Lincs Rally, an event which qualified for the national Castrol/Autosport series. Trouble started before the rally because the organizers had stated that competitors had to sign on at least half-an-hour before the start, under threat of non-starting – a threat they were ready to implement as there were several reserves ready to step in at the last moment. I went alone, since Graham had worked late the night before and I wanted him to enjoy what sleep he could get. When we eventually reported at the start some ten minutes or so before the 'off', we found our number had been re-allocated and we were barred from starting.

Number one rule is to understand the problem: it was simply that the organizers had meant *both* competitors had to be present. The next rule is to appreciate what can be done. Obviously all the organizers could offer was the next vacant starting number. Third, we had to persuade them to implement this possibility. This took the longest time, because all the while we were arguing and suggesting compromises they were allocating vacant numbers to the reserves. Eventually we came to terms and number 47 was the next vacant hole in the entry list.

This sort of situation can be extremely demoralizing for a driver: not only that, but if a driver senses even remotely that a co-driver has allowed this to happen through neglect, it causes a very quick breakdown in the relationship inside the car. Once again my job was to ignore the potential tension and think clearly about the new situation. The advantages were various, but essentially as follows: it was a damp morning and any slippery stages early in the rally would become drier and might favour us; furthermore, assuming that we did not suffer blockages from competitors, we had the excellent situation of knowing exactly what times the early runners were taking on the stages, without any chance of their knowing our times. In fact this is exactly what happened: on the first stage Graham was twenty seconds quicker than the next man and forty quicker than George Hill who came second on the rally overall. And at half time the leading few competitors had to leave for the afternoon stages before our first-half score was announced. It was almost too good to be true. Moral: never prejudge a situation simply because it looks like going wrong!

The 1975 Tour of Lincs. A surprise victory which began with an argument at the start (Graham Lepley and Martin with a 2-litre RS 1600)

Always be on the look-out that things might go right! A strangely worded section in the regulation for an old Witsend Rally gave Nick Ward and me a win when we never deserved it at all. The rally was decided on road penalties which included the element of the number of minutes lost on a selective section, and should a tie result then the number of minutes and seconds lost on the selective would be considered. We lost three minutes on the ordinary road sections and two 115 minutes fifty-eight seconds on the selective, while the next man, Roy Edwards, lost two minutes on the road and three minutes two seconds on the selective. To me the situation was clear. His two minutes on the road made him the winner and our three the second-place men. But no! By adding the three and the two from our scores we equalled the two and the three of Edwards, so they had to consider the selective times to decide the result. This gave us the victory. What I should have realized before the rally was that the selective section might count twice in the final results, and therefore we should try specially hard on that section. We were lucky on two counts: first that we had a good time on the selective without realizing how important it might be, and second that the selective was not just a little bit shorter. If the selective had been, say, a hundred yards shorter, we would each have taken four or five seconds less. We would have taken two minutes fifty-three seconds, Edwards two minutes fifty-seven seconds. Had this been so, the tie-deciding aspect of the selective would never have come into operation, because we would have had greater road penalties in the first place.

Again, on another rally in south-east England, Tony Maslen and I were taken off the route, by some crass mis-navigation on my part (it was always extremely tricky just there). We were stranded with the car bogged down completely. Quite by coincidence cars were stuck elsewhere on that section and the rally was stopped at the previous control. By complete chance Tony and I eventually drove to the finish of the rally to hand in our time cards, and found we had won. Nine times out of ten a driver will be right to throw a fit and lose interest when things go wrong, but every tenth time there is some benefit to be obtained that you would never dream about.

Interpreting regulations is the ultimate challenge in self-confidence. And funnily enough more trouble in interpreting regulations comes on the Internationals than on club events, where many ambiguous matters can be resolved simply by looking at the RAC's standard regulations. This is my weak point. I admire other co-drivers who can read a set of regulations, spot immediately the things the regulations do not say, take advantage of an omission, and succeed. I almost break out into a cold sweat clocking in late at a time control on an International even when I have read a hundred times that there is no penalty for late arrival! I studied the regulations for the 1975 RAC Rally and discovered that there were curious circumstances at the rest halts. These were of little concern until we heard that there were no *parcs fermés* at these places, so we could drive to the control to clock in, then drive away to carry out service in a convenient and uncrowded place, before driving back to clock out. It seemed that if you clocked in either early or on time, you were allowed to clock out up to your maximum of one-hour late, yet if you clocked in late, the regulations required you to clock out on standard time. We wanted to be certain that any essential time-consuming work would not have to be disturbed by driving back to the control, and also that any sudden congestion at the control would not prevent our clocking out on time, which would be serious if we had clocked in late. We therefore clocked in first and then drove away to the service point rather than carry out all our work first and then clock in. What I noticed on arriving at the control point was that the marshals were in a café and completely unable to see whether the relevant cars were in the control or not, so that it was not necessary to bring the rally car back to the control area for clocking out at all. The thought of clocking out with the car four miles away is very daunting, though it was nice to know this could be done if things were really desperate.

We were once really desperate on the Scottish. Chris and I were driving the good old Datsun Violet, and we were really scratching to make any headway at all on the rally. The car's attributes were wasted on that event: its reliability was to no avail and the event was shorter

Datsun Violet. Chris and Martin scratching for a position even in the top ten on the 1975 Scottish Rally. Eventually they managed seventh place overall, but only by virtue of some brinkmanship with the regulations

than usual anyway. On the final day we needed all the good times we could get, and the most important stage was Culbin. This was about forty-five miles away from the re-start, and it was a perfect opportunity for the organizers to check whether competitors were exceeding the forty-miles-an-hour average speed limit. We knew this well, and as we drove nearer and nearer to the stage we scoured the horizons for a possible secret check. There was none. But could the organizers deduce from the time of arrival at the start of the special stage whether we had exceeded the permitted average speed on the road? Against all the odds, the regulations stated that they could not. For us this was vital, because the only good time at Culbin is the time of the first car through. The surface of the stage is very sandy and is cut up badly by the passage of rally cars. We wanted to be the first car through, and the only way was to overtake all the other cars on the road section leading up to the stage. It was obvious that other people were playing safe and keeping within the forty-mile average speed limit. One by one we overtook the cars ahead of us, and we arrived at the stage first. We felt really bold, but boldness started to turn to unease when other drivers thought we were wrong – and said so. It was an interesting situation. The deed was done, there was no going back.

In the end my nerve broke. Robin Turvey, the Opel team liaison man, asked if I was absolutely certain that there wasn't some sub-sub-clause that covered this situation. I said bravely there wasn't, but as we drove away I reached for my regulations once again and opened them inside the road book so Chris would not notice what I was doing! In fact we had been right, we gained what for us was a place that we wanted, although we still only finished seventh, and the whole episode was of minor importance.

You as co-driver/navigator are the decision-maker of the team. Take confidence in what you decide, convey your confidence at all times to your driver – but never become so rigid in your self-confidence that you cannot take advantage of unexpected situations.

John Davenport and Chris in the Jolly Club Lancia (1969 Gremlin Rally)

12 *Teams*
By CHRIS SCLATER

Looking back over my career so far at the variety of cars I have driven and the teams I have been involved with can only teach me lessons beneficial to the future. No team is perfect. None would claim to be. Probably the most efficient organizations are the small self-contained ones. Decisions can be made on the spot with no recourse to a higher authority. Politics can be kept out of the job of trying to win rallies. Unfortunately few people can win rallies without reliance on either a sponsorship or a motor manufacturer's money. As soon as big money from outside sources is involved, responsibilities are increased.

The most enjoyable period of my rallying was in the early days when I was operating on my own, working during the day earning money, and working at home on the rally car in the evenings and at weekends. I had to answer to nobody and nothing except my own ambitions. As soon as the ambitions became greater somebody else's support was required, either in the form of volunteer help, sponsorship money – or both.

The first sponsor I had was the Allard Motor Company. I worked for them and they supported my entries. The first time I drove someone else's car was in 1969 on the Gremlin Rally in Wales. This was a rare outing for me on a *Motoring News* Championship Road Rally. It happened like this. Colin Malkin was to drive a Lancia Fulvia for the Jolly Club in Britain under the leadership of Oliver Speight – an ex-competitions manager at Dunlop. Colin was away at the time and John Davenport suggested to Oliver that I should be offered the drive. This was the night before the rally and I hadn't seen the rally car – let alone driven any Fulvia – and this one was left-hand drive.

Naturally I accepted the drive. Unfortunately, as so often happens when you are over-keen to prove yourself, it ended with a small excursion up a bank and consequent damage to the steering. I drove another event in the Lancia later in the year, and that time the clutch failed. In fact a lot of people drove for Oliver Speight – Tony Fall, Pat Moss, Mike Hibbert, John Bloxham and George Hill, as well as Colin and myself. It was a team full of good intentions and enthusiasm but lacking the backing to be really successful.

My next association, which lasted longer, was probably more turbulent but was certainly more successful. It was with Cal Withers. Cal realized that his hobby of rallying could be put to good commercial

The 1971 Circuit of Ireland Rally – the J. C. Withers Rally Team in full force!

advantage by assisting the sale of competition parts for rally cars from his car-breaking business in Cheshire. I first met Cal at Ford's Competition Department in early 1970. I was looking for support for my rallying and started to chat to him. The result was an offer to drive his Escort on the Circuit of Ireland Rally that Easter.

I still had my own Escort and was quite happy to carry on preparing myself and driving rallies with sponsorship. We hit upon a deal whereby he would provide support along these lines. The Circuit was entered on a very low level. The Escort TC at 1600 c.c. was a reliable car and the only service I had in Ireland was a friend of my co-driver with his Cortina carrying what spares I had. Fords had entered Roger Clark and Adrian Boyd and I was able to borrow a bit of help from them. The result was astonishing when we considered the outlay: second place behind Roger – admittedly about fifteen minutes behind his Group 6 car – but Withers already had a return on his modest investment.

The next event – the Welsh International – gave the same result: second, this time behind Will Sparrow after a real battle with the Mini driver. In fact I finished runner-up to Sparrow in the RAC Championship that year. Withers was still running his own car for Roy Fidler to drive, and supporting others as well. He enjoyed being involved and seeing his name carried on successful cars, though perhaps the overall commitment was too much for the size of the business.

Sometimes the business interfered with the rallying in the worst way. A typical example of this was on the Circuit of Ireland in 1971. I broke a rear spring on the second day while in the lead. We had to drive a couple of stages with the old spring before reaching the service car. We changed the spring for a second-hand spare, knowing that Cal had got two new competition ones in his van which would be a few stages further on.

Because of the strain of driving with one broken, the other spring went on the next stage. Okay. We could fit the two new ones and all would be well again. But on reaching Cal we discovered he had sold

Right: Successful Sclater/Withers combination winning the 1971 Scottish Rally

the two new springs to another competitor. The result was a total of a hundred miles of stages with a broken rear spring until we managed to make up two new ones. It probably cost us first place.

I could understand Cal wanting to make some money from his involvement, but to sell the only springs when you have a car leading the rally doesn't make sense. The lesson was learnt. I made sure that either my own service car carried the parts or that I knew certain items would be reserved for me.

Cal Withers was a very valuable stepping stone in my career. He supported not only my rallying activities for two years but also entries in Rallycross, Mexico Racing and Stadium Racing. 1971 was my best year in terms of results – winning the Scottish Rally, several nationals and the British Championship. Cal and I had numerous arguments about who had helped who most but I think it worked out fairly evenly in the end.

The same organization also gave me the chance to drive a Datsun 240Z – the Big D – in the TAP Rally in 1972. Anybody who hasn't sampled a 240 has really missed one of the great experiences of rallying!

I took Dutchman Bob de Jong as my co-driver, and although the outcome wasn't too satisfactory, because of a head gasket failure, we thoroughly enjoyed ourselves. There was one amusing incident after the fibreglass bonnet had flown open and blocked our vision on a fast main road. I stopped safely and we made a temporary repair with elastic straps. Jumping back into the car we nearly knocked ourselves out. The bonnet had made a big dent in the roof and we hadn't noticed because of the worry of losing vision at a hundred and fifty kilometres an hour. When the shock had passed and we had knocked the roof up again, we just sat in the car laughing. In fact, we were still laughing thirty kilometres later at the control and nobody could understand why! It was probably just the release of a lot of tension.

The RAC Rally in 1972 was my first drive for Clarke & Simpson Ltd, a company no longer in the motor business but at that time one of the leading competitors in rallying. I drove their own Escort BDA. For the first time, in a rally, I was to drive an Escort that didn't belong to me. It seemed strange not to be worrying about the preparation or the tyres – or, more important, the money. I obviously benefited from the situation because I drove better than ever before, lying third at the Severn Bridge after about thirty stages. Unfortunately retirement was forced on us soon afterwards when the engine failed.

That team at Clarke & Simpson was good. The cars were well prepared under the supervision of David Sutton, and the whole set-up was small enough to be independent and yet professional enough to produce good results. At that time, they were one of the most successful of the private teams, being able to call on such drivers as Timo Makinen, Mike Hibbert and Barry Lee. Eighteen months later I was to drive for Clarke & Simpson again in Spain and Portugal.

Following that RAC drive, and possibly because of it, I was awarded the first Kleber Wheelbase Scholarship; the prize was a works-built Escort and financial assistance toward entry on four nominated rallies, as well as free tyres. Considering that I was struggling to find enough money to run my car, this award came at the right time and would certainly give me the opportunity for my best season yet.

Ford were involved with the scholarship in that they provided the Escort and offered to give service back-up on as many events as possible. The events nominated for the car were the Monte, Acropolis, Sherry and RAC. In addition, I would be driving my own Escort on the Firestone in Spain, Boucles de Spa in Belgium, and the Welsh and Scottish Rallies. I also had driven on the TAP Rally and the BNU in South Africa in Datsuns, and the Cyprus Rally in a Marina for British Leyland. A very busy year.

The involvement with Fords was good. On the Monte and Acropolis Rallies I received full service, and for the Sherry Rally I borrowed a practice car and a service car with mechanic Eric Bigwood. It was very generous help, and also fabulous experience for me to be rallying with Peter Ashcroft, Mick Jones and the mechanics at Boreham – definitely the premier British team and arguably the best in Europe. Britain produces the best mechanics and co-drivers, if nothing else!

I have already described my participation in the Monte, but the work that goes on behind the scenes in a works team is largely unknown to the general public. Soon after the RAC Rally, one of the team's co-drivers will go to France, with or without his driver, to drive over the route. He will find out if new roads are to be used and will plan the format of the rally. Time schedules are worked out and preliminary tyre requirements can be fed back to Dunlop.

On a rally like the Monte, changing conditions can be a deciding factor. Ford use a team of ice-note crews who pass over the stages before the rally arrives. Each crew will deal with three or four stages and check them several times. A good judgement of general conditions can be made by checking at the same time of day that the rally passes.

Driving with Kleber Wheelbase and Ford. Chris winning the 1973 Sherry Rally with Henry Liddon co-driving

For instance, water might be running across the road from an overflowing stream; it might freeze at night and then thaw in the day. A copy of the pace notes to be used will be marked to show where the ice or snow occurs, and these will be checked up to within a few hours of the car arriving. The information is passed back to the Ford headquarters in a hotel at Monte Carlo to give Dunlop an idea of tyre requirements at each special test.

Each service point is normally close to a telephone box, or an hotel or restaurant, and the mechanics will be kept up to date with information. When the rally cars arrive at the service point before the start of each test they are given a copy of the marked pace notes and an indication of the percentage of ice and snow on that test. The driver will then make a decision on his tyre requirements and the servicing will carry on as usual. Sometimes there might have to be a further tyre change allowed for at the end of the test, if the conditions on the next road section are drastically different. All this progress must be fed back to the team's headquarters so that contingency plans can be made if there are any serious problems with the car. So the team's co-driver has to take notes of telephone numbers at the location of the service points and work out a schedule for the service crews as well as the ice-note crews.

Meanwhile, back in England, the Rally Manager is booking hotels, boat tickets, insurance, and making sure that the car preparation is on schedule. Last-minute tyre testing may also have to be carried out.

On the Monte there may be five or six service cars and two tyre trucks. A lot of personnel and a lot of organization. This sort of organization takes a weight off the rally driver's shoulders and can give him tremendous confidence. Driving in a team of this sort can be an instant psychological advantage.

Driving with British Leyland as I did in Cyprus and later on the Rothmans 747 Rally in Jamaica was a different experience. The

Chris on the 1973 Cyprus Rally with British Leyland

underlying theme of all Leyland's rallying activities is promotion. A promotional programme is arranged around the rally so that success on the event itself is of secondary importance. The standard of car preparation is very high as well, although the two cars that I drove for Leyland were built locally with parts supplied from the Abingdon Competitions Department.

In Cyprus I drove a 1300 Marina and in Jamaica a 1300 Mini Clubman GT. The Cyprus Rally followed five days after the Sherry Rally in Spain, which I won with Henry Liddon in the Kleber Wheelbase Escort. So our recce for Cyprus was very rushed, but even so we were involved in the Leyland promotional machine. Brian Culcheth, their permanent driver for many years – in fact since the days of the Mini successes – spearheads the team's rallying involvement. In Cyprus a film was being made and, both before and after the rally, Brian spent several weeks visiting Leyland dealers on the island and demonstrating his Marina rally car, giving talks and showing films.

On the recce we all gave away Marina hats in the villages en route. In fact they were so popular we just threw them out of the window – had we stopped, the kids would have torn us apart! By the start of the rally everyone on the island seemed to be wearing these hats.

This accent on public relations naturally brings the drivers in close contact with the advertising and publicity side of the company. I feel this is a good thing, because it makes them realize the reasons behind factory involvement in competition, although it shouldn't, and doesn't, override the effort put into success on the rallies themselves.

At the end of 1973 I was offered a drive in the Datsun team for the RAC Rally. Although it had been intended that I should drive the Kleber Escort, the fact that the Datsun offer had been made vindicated the whole intention of the scholarship. I accepted the drive which was to be the beginning of a two-year involvement with Datsun. Not only an involvement as a driver, but also on the testing and development side. Out of this came a trip to Japan and a good result on the Total Rally in South Africa, as well as victory in the Manufacturers' Team competition on the RAC Rally.

Dealing with the Japanese is a difficult business, because their culture and way of life is so different from ours. With no strong history in engineering and invention, the manufacture of motor cars – and particularly of competition cars – is carried out very much according to the book, or with recourse to a computer. Very little in the way of adaptation to accord with personal instinct or feeling is built into a car. It took the Japanese a long time to understand just what rallying was, but once they did they became a force to be reckoned with.

A situation occurred before the 1973 RAC Rally which illustrates the sort of problems we faced. We were testing the 240Z rally cars at a forest in Wales with the idea of getting used to driving them, and testing different tyres. After a few laps of the circuit that we had laid out it became clear to all three drivers (Tony Fall, Harry Källström and myself) that the brakes were unsuitable for the RAC Rally. The rear braking effort was totally inadequate; with a 240Z this is a serious fault because it is a 'straight-on' car at the best of times.

When we confronted the chief rally engineer with our thoughts and suggested he should rectify the situation before the rally, it caused a major upset. First, for him to make a modification without the backing of the testing department back in Tokyo would be against all company methods. Second, the computer had designed the brakes – and the computer must be right. He didn't tell us that the brakes had been designed for normal tarmac driving, however. It wasn't until Tony Fall had taken him in his rally car and come close to an accident that he finally agreed to allow the modification to be carried out.

The next obstacle was to get the work done. The Japanese mechanics could bolt on a ready-designed and manufactured part, knew all the torque settings of the bolts, knew where to use Locktite and how long the part would last, but were not geared up to modify and adapt. So Tony and I had to contact Lockheed and seek their advice and assistance. Eventually we got hold of brake servo kits to fit into the rear brake lines of the three rally cars. The Japanese managed to fit them according to Lockheed's instructions and the brake balance proved to be very good.

Thorough servicing was always carried out during the rally. Whatever the weather or conditions of the car, the Japanese mechanics

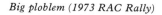

Big ploblem (1973 RAC Rally)

The Datsun team for the 1974 RAC Rally

always set to on a thorough routine inspection as soon as the car stopped at a service point. You could always count on the reliability of these vehicles, and certainly this was how their reputation was made, especially on the long-distance events like the East African Safari.

After the 240Z the Violet (710) was used for rallying, and this was the car I campaigned in the British Rally Championship of 1974. We were sent the first one built, for appraisal. My job, apart from driving, was to carry on with the development and feed back information on our progress to Japan. One of the modifications we carried out was the fitting of an anti-roll bar on the rear suspension. The Japanese could see no point in this and said that their test driver was producing slower times with the bar fitted than without. What they didn't tell us was that they were testing the car on an oval track with a very hard surface. Naturally, twisting rally roads would give different effects. At the RAC Rally all the cars had anti-rollbars fitted and drivers were asked to test with and without them. Better results were obtained with the bar, I'm pleased to say. In fact we won the Manufacturers' Team Prize that year.

I also drove for the big rival of Datsun – that other Japanese team, Toyota. That two cars and teams emanating from the same country and city could be so different was difficult to understand at first. But the Toyota set-up is now handled by Europeans, led in fact by one of the most successful Swedish rallies drivers, Ove Andersson – a man who has won, among many others, the Monte Carlo and Safari Rallies, and who has dedicated his life to making the Toyota a successful competition car. I drove a Corolla 1600 on the RAC in 1975. On this event all the mechanics were European – Swedish, German or British. The cars had been built in Brussels at Andersson's rallying headquarters. My car was the best handling machine I had driven and, for a 1600, was very quick. In fact we had worked up to fifth place, challenging for fourth, when I slid into a ditch on the last night of the rally. We managed to get out eventually and still won the class, although it took a long time for me to forget the disappointment I felt at not killing a few giants with a fabulous little car. This was certainly the most enjoyable RAC that I had ever driven in.

Working with this team was fabulous. It was relatively small and yet had the right sort of financial backing to be completely professional. The other drivers on the RAC were Hannu Mikkola and Ove Andersson himself, who continued to be the two permanent drivers in 1976. The spirit amongst the mechanics in the Toyota team was fantastic. They understood rallying and what was required of them, and were completely dedicated to building successful cars. I had a feeling they were totally inspired by Ove's determination.

The fabulous Toyota Corolla (Chris and Martin, 1975 RAC Rally)

Rallying is a sport where determination is one of the most important qualities in the competitor. Success only comes after battles with your bank balance, other competitors and yourself. I have threatened to stop rallying a million times but have found it impossible to replace the excitement and satisfaction that the sport can give. Few people are lucky enough to be involved at a professional level with the professional teams. It was my ambition from the beginning to get there, and without any particular advantages but with a lot of luck I fulfilled that ambition.

I hope you do.